ISBN 978-1-331-85759-4
PIBN 10242943

Forgotten Books is a registered trademark of FB &c Ltd.
Copyright © 2015 FB &c Ltd.
FB &c Ltd, Dalton House, 60 Windsor Avenue, London, SW19 2RR.
Company number 08720141. Registered in England and Wales.

For support please visit www.forgottenbooks.com

1 MONTH OF
FREE
READING

at

www.ForgottenBooks.com

By purchasing this book you are eligible for one month membership to ForgottenBooks.com, giving you unlimited access to our entire collection of over 700,000 titles via our web site and mobile apps.

To claim your free month visit: www.forgottenbooks.com/free242943

Similar Books Are Available from
www.forgottenbooks.com

Beautiful Joe
An Autobiography, by Marshall Saunders

Theodore Roosevelt, an Autobiography
by Theodore Roosevelt

Napoleon
A Biographical Study, by Max Lenz

Up from Slavery
An Autobiography, by Booker T. Washington

Gotama Buddha
A Biography, Based on the Canonical Books of the Theravādin, by Kenneth J. Saunders

Plato's Biography of Socrates
by A. E. Taylor

Cicero
A Biography, by Torsten Petersson

Madam Guyon
An Autobiography, by Jeanne Marie Bouvier De La Motte Guyon

The Writings of Thomas Jefferson
by Thomas Jefferson

Thomas Skinner, M.D.
A Biographical Sketch, by John H. Clarke

Saint Thomas Aquinas of the Order of Preachers (1225-1274)
A Biographical Study of the Angelic Doctor, by Placid Conway

Recollections of the Rev. John Johnson and His Home
An Autobiography, by Susannah Johnson

Biographical Sketches in Cornwall, Vol. 1 of 3
by R. Polwhele

Autobiography of John Francis Hylan, Mayor of New York
by John Francis Hylan

The Autobiography of Benjamin Franklin
The Unmutilated and Correct Version, by Benjamin Franklin

James Mill
A Biography, by Alexander Bain

George Washington
An Historical Biography, by Horace E. Scudder

Florence Nightingale
A Biography, by Irene Cooper Willis

Marse Henry
An Autobiography, by Henry Watterson

Autobiography and Poems
by Charlotte E. Linden

DYING AT THE TOP;

OR,

The Moral and Spiritual Condition of the Young Men of America.

BY

REV. JOSEPH WADDELL CLOKEY, D.D.,

PASTOR OF THE

FIRST PRESBYTERIAN CHURCH

OF NEW ALBANY, INDIANA.

REVISED AND ENLARGED.

Price: Paper, 25 Cents; Cloth, 50 Cents.

"There is nothing covered that shall not be revealed."—*Christ.*

PUBLISHED BY

YOUNG MEN'S ERA PUBLISHING CO.,

10 ARCADE COURT, CHICAGO, ILL.

1890.

CONTENTS.

DEDICATION.

———

To the Young Men's Christian Association of the United States, whose work constitutes one of the greatest movements of this great century, this Book is dedicated, in the hope that the facts presented in it may stimulate its members to a still greater zeal in the redeeming of young men to the morality and faith of the Lord Jesus Christ.

J. W. CLOKEY.

PREFACE.

The original form of this work was an address delivered before the Indiana State Sunday School Union, at its convention in Columbus, Ind., held June 21, 22 and 23, 1887. The address, published in the proceedings of the convention, and delivered subsequently in different places, has awakened so much interest by the facts it presents, that it has been thought advisable to enlarge it, and issue it in a form for general circulation. The title, Dying at the Top, was the outgrowth of a real heart-sorrow. In my yard at home stands what is left of a favorite apricot tree. For years it had stood there, the very symbol of life and vigor. Its beautiful blossoms were among the earliest harbingers of spring, and the fruit that soon followed the falling of the bloom, was delicious in the extreme. The tree was our pride and delight. But one day I saw that the very topmost branches had withered; and I said, "Ah, our apricot is death-smitten; it is *dying at the top.*" These top branches were cut off, but the next season the next highest withered. And now there is not enough life left in the tree to mature what few blossoms it puts forth. On examination *worms were found at the root;* they had worked their way up *under the bark*, and though the outside seemed firm and healthy, the tree was almost girdled by the unseen pests, and death was inevitable.

From the dying of the tree-top came the theme, and from the theme came the following pages. Before me now stands the Human Tree, and it is with a sadness approaching dejection, that I say: *"It is dying at the top."*

APOLOGY.

This little work has now been before the public for a year. The number of copies sold has not been very great, but there is evidence that those that have been sold have been widely circulated. They have gone into every State in the Union; and been everywhere in the hands of those who are best able to judge of the truthfulness of the statements made.

The author, in giving the work to the world, did it with much hesitation, knowing how liable statistics are to err; and how often the facts gathered from a few communities may not prove to be true of the country at large.

At the present writing, the saddest thing about the work is that it has told the truthful story of the whole land. Not a single person has arisen to deny its correctness; while from Maine to California, and from Oregon to Florida, letter after letter has come, saying " It is all true." If it is all true, and true everywhere, then American society, from ocean to ocean, is suspended over an abyss, and it will require the engineering skill of the best elements in Church and State to keep us from falling into depths of distress along side of which the taxation of England, in the old colonial days, and the slavery of the South, were but baubles.

The troubles growing up between nation and nation, and State and State, over their material relations, have been to a great extent the incidents of human progress, where the strong body of our national manhood has been throwing off the shackles of its old-time bondage. But corruption in the morals of our people is the incident of a deep-seated disease, whose cancerous properties will sooner or later bring us into troubles worse than war or oppression, unless we correct them.

When dangers exist in our domestic or national life,' it is the duty of the true citizen to point them out. If our neighbor's property is threatened with the flames, we will be guilty of incendiarism if we do not cry "Fire! Fire!" If the lives of our fellow citizens are in jeopardy, we are in spirit murderers if we lift no voice of alarm; and if there is a condition of morals and manners among any classes of our people, threatening the prosperity and permanency of the Republic, we are not patriots if we hold our peace.

"Dying at the Top" is a cry of alarm. Perhaps the cry is a too noisy one for those who are accustomed to moving delicately. But is it not better for all that an alarm be raised than that we should be silent in the presence of danger?

Two objections have been urged against this work, and they are noticed here in the hope that they may be removed. The first is that it touches on the social evil.

But why should licentiousness be exempted from exposure? Is it no serious evil? Is it a social disease that will correct itself if it is let alone? Are its dangers not to be met and mastered in the same way that other immoralities have been met and mastered?

The history of reform has shown that no iniquity has ever been subdued till the facts connected with it were torn from their secrecy and laid open to the gaze of the world. The reformation of the 16th century was made possible only because the reformers of France and Germany told to all mankind the secret doings of the papacy, in its sale of indulgences, in its inquisitions and autos-dä-fé, and in the horrible transactions of a corrupted priesthood in the nunneries and monasteries of the Middle Ages. The literature of three and four hundred years ago is full of revelations that would make the prudishly pure of our day blush, but which did their work in bringing to the knowledge of the people the dangers that underlay all European society.

The history of the Reformation in England under

the Wesleys is the history of the exposure of the excesses of the day, and the consequent re-action against them.

One of Great Britain's noble charities is found in her "Ragged Schools." These schools originated with Dr. Guthrie, who first himself went down among the wretched haunts and homes of the poor of Edinburg, and then startled his country by relating what he discovered of the squalor and vice of masses of the people.

The secret of the power of the writings of Charles Dickens lies in his opening to the sunlight the wrongs perpetrated on children and on the laboring classes in the name of education and employment.

The sensitive people of this country were greatly shocked at the revelations made some time since in the *Pall Mall Gazette* of London, of corruptions among certain of the English nobility. W. L. Stead, the editor, was thought to be a species of monster who was ready to cast upon society any obscene material, provided it would contribute to his exchequer. But after the first excitement had subsided, and we were willing to be reasonable in our judgment, the reading public learned two things. First, that Mr. Stead was a great philanthropist, and that it was in the interest of suffering humanity that he unearthed and exposed those dreadful scandals. He says of himself in "Books which have Influenced Me": "I have never ceased for one moment to rejoice that I was a journalist, and at the same time to feel weighed down with a sense of my utter incapacity to even approach the ideal of a journalist's mission in these later days. What is that mission? Let Victor Hugo speak. He is describing what Gwymplaine said to himself when he accepted his position as peer: 'The people are silence. I shall be the advocate of that silence. I will speak for the dumb. I will speak of the small to the great, and of the feeble to the strong. That is the aim of my destiny. . . I am predestinated. I have a mission. I shall be lord of the poor. I shall speak for the despairing, silent ones. I shall interpret this stammering; I

shall interpret the grumblings, the murmurings, the tu-
mults of the crowds, the complaints ill-pronounced, the
unintelligible voices, and all these cries of beasts that,
through ignorance and through suffering, man is forced
to utter.　　　　　　I will be the word to the people.　I
will be the bleeding mouth whence the gag is snatched
out.　I will speak everything.'"

W. L. Stead spoke "everything" for the "despairing,
silent ones," and society soon learned a second thing, that
the English Parliament had heard his cries and come to
the relief of England's unprotected girls.　To-day they
are guarded by vigilant laws as they have never before
been, and philanthropic women are watching with re-
newed vigilance to break up the once almost unnoticed
and unchallenged traffic in young girls, which was carried on between England and the Continent of Europe.

The writer of this work does not plead for the pub-
lication of the minute details of any vice; only that the
vice should be recognized and properly exposed from
all those places where truth told can be made to prevail.

The sensitiveness that takes offense at such expo-
sures needs to be reconstructed.　It is not a mark either
of depth or purity of character.　Show me an audience
where the people exchange glances and shrug their
shoulders, and look sour when the speaker utters his
earnest words against uncleanness of life, and I will show
you a people who have a far greater experimental knowledge of certain nameless sins than they would dare to
make public.

Strong men and women who are conscious of their
personal integrity, and who crave to know where a vice
lurks that they may the better smite it, can listen with
dignity to any delicate disclosure of sin, and pass out
without any sense of injury.

There is a remarkable passage in the 90th Psalm:
"Thou hast set our iniquities before Thee, our secret sins
in the light of Thy countenance."　The vices of society
are "in the light of God's countenance," and instead of
spending His time blushing and looking ashamed, He

flies to our rescue in the gift of His own dear Son. And so we should consent to have the sins of the world brought into the light of our countenance and kept there, until by breaking our bodies and shedding our blood, we blot the facts of vice out of our sight by blotting out the vice itself.

. In giving "Dying at the Top" to the world, the author has been called a "pessimist." A pessimist, according to the popular understanding of the word, is a man of sour and gloomy turn of mind, who seeks no sunspots in life, but gropes round among its shadows and sewers, bringing to the light of day dark and wretched doings which really have no serious bearing on social and national life, but which he thinks are omens of coming disaster. He is a mole, burrowing under the ground, unconscious of God's bright and glorious world above; a bat that shuts itself away in some corner, and flaps its wings only when night's shadows are over the world; an owl, silent in the glory of reigning day, and hooting its dismal prophesies out of the darkness. An "optimist," by the same popular interpretation, is a bright, cheerful soul, who keeps his face and his soul always in the light of God's countenance; who finds nothing but hope everywhere and in everything; who reasons that God reigns, and God knows how to run a world so as to make all things work together for the good of His creatures; who turns his face away from the hidden thing of darkness, refusing to think of them or tell others of them, because there is no real danger in them. With him health alone is catching, and purity and holiness hold the key to the situation. He is a lark, up by the earliest dawn, to soar high in heaven's pure air, and to sing his sweet notes far out of and above these doleful and dismal things of earth. He is an eagle, whose eye is fixed on the sky, and which, mounting from crag to crag, from high in the air spreads its splendid wings for the bosom of the sun.

A genuine pessimist is one who, after he has looked on all sides of the facts and problems of the hour, con-

cludes that the trend of events is, on the surface and in
the depths of human society, toward the darkness. He
sees no reason for hope; hence his song is a doleful
one, the outcome of a soul in trouble and despair. The
true optimist is one who, after taking the same general
view of events, sees both in the depths and on the surface evidence that the world is growing better every day.
He rises from the study of even the darkest pages of the
day with hope. He says the Christ has proved the
Master in a thousand crises and He will prove Master in
this. With his face turned full on the doings of the
papacy and the saloon and the anarchist; with the full
knowledge of the perils of the modern city, of emigra-
tion, of the corporation and of trusts, he still says with
Galileo, "The world does move." In this definition of
terms, the writer is a decided optimist. On the top of
that long train of freight cars, a young man is running
backward, and if he keeps on running, he will plunge off
the end of the train and be ruined. But the *train* thun-
ders on; immense products thunder on with it; even the
young brakesman on the top moves forward faster than
he does backward, and when he falls, falls farther ahead.
Human society is this moving train. Not for a moment,
in the long records of the past, has its wheels ceased or
turned to move backward, and whilst thousands to-day
resist the power of the onward movement and become
vicious in their lives, even they fall farther forward than
the vicious of a hundred or a thousand years ago. The
cruelties of the old Roman amphi-theatres are gone, never
to return. Men and beasts are no longer fattened to
slaughter one another for the amusement of fine socie-
ties. Splendid paganism lives only in the ruins of its
Pantheon and Parthenon. Its mythic deities are silent
on Olympus, while the Cross stands in the centre of the
Colosseum, and the voice and songs of the Christian
missionary are heard where Jove hurled his thunder-
bolts and Saturn shook the trident of the seas. In
modern Europe an inquisition is impossible. The world
to-day sees the thumb-screw and the stocks only in

some Eden Musee, where the horrors of the by-gones are exhibited in figures of plaster-of-Paris to remind the present that torture for honest convictions had ever existed.

The low forms of amusement and vice that, even one hundred and fifty years ago, flung defiance before an offended public, to-day exist in concealment, and are indulged in, in dread of the supreme fiat of Law. Lecky, in speaking of the coarseness of manners of the eighteenth century in England, says: "Each king lived public-ly with his mistresses, and the immorality of their courts was accompanied by nothing of that refinement or grace which has often cast a softening veil over much deeper and more general corruption."

A queen like that of George II. is not possible to-day at the Court of England, who, though virtuous herself, "passed through life jesting on the vices of her husband and of his ministers, with the coarseness of a trooper, receiving from her husband the earliest and fullest accounts of every new love affair in which he was engaged, and prepared to welcome each new mistress, provided only she could herself keep the first place in his judgment and confidence."

The young men of to-day, though reckless, are respectable in their amusements along side of those of one hundred and fifty years ago. Bull-baiting, bear-baiting and cock-fighting were the open every-day entertainment of the youth of all classes in society. What would we think now of such an advertisement as this, which was common in London at the beginning of the 18th century? "A mad bull to be dressed up with fire-works and turned loose in the game place, a dog to be dressed up with fire-works over him, a bear to be let loose at the same time, and a cat to be tied to the bull's tail; a mad bull dressed up with fire-works to be baited." In 1712, in London, young men from the nobility organized a club, and called themselves the "mohawks" Lecky says of them that "they were accustomed to sally out drunk into the streets to hunt the passers-by and to subject them in mere wantonness to the most atrocious outrages. One of their favorite amusements, called 'tip-ping the lion,' was to squeeze the nose of their victim flat upon his face and to bore out his eyes with their fingers. Among them were the 'sweaters,' who formed a circle round their prisoner and pricked him with their swords till he sank exhausted to the ground; the 'dancing masters,' so called from their skill in making men caper by thrusting swords into their legs; the 'tumblers,' whose favorite amusement was to set women on their heads and commit various indecencies and barbarities on the limbs that were exposed. Maid-servants, as they opened their masters' doors, were waylaid, beaten, and their faces cut. Matrons, inclosed in barrels, were rolled down the steep and stony incline of Snow Hill. Watchmen were unmercifully beaten and their noses slit."

When one reads such accounts as these, given both by Lecky and McCarthy, he turns to his own times with comfort, and even with the recklessness of our American youth before him, thanks God that his day is the best day in the history of mankind.

So the author sends this little work to the world with his face towards the sunshine, assured that the forces are present with us to conquer our country for Christ, provided the facts are made known and the evils of our day exposed.

The facts and figures in the following pages have been selected with the greatest possible care. None of them have been taken on mere rumor. What has been given in reference to prisons and crime has come from personal examination of documents. The figures relating to church attendance, and to the young man in the saloon and bagnio, have been furnished by Secretaries of the Young Men's Christian Association, by pastors and physicians, all of whom are men of standing and reputation in the communities where they live.

There has been no selection of material to make a bad case. The author has been controlled by a desire to under-estimate rather than to over-estimate. "Dying at the To " is an honest attem t to tell the sim le truth.

DYING AT THE TOP.

CHAPTER I.

AT THE TOP.

In the progress of human affairs no character has risen higher in importance and influence than the *young man.* It might almost be said that he has made history what it is. What great crisis in the story of the nations has there been when he did not come to the front as soldier, statesman, or reformer? When God would change the kingdom of the Hebrews from a theocracy to a monarchy, it was Saul, "a choice young man," who was selected for the throne.

When David first appeared at the Hebrew court he was addressed by the king, "Whose son art thou, thou young man?" It was as a young man that he won the hearts of all Israel by his valor in the field, and at the age of thirty-one he ascended the throne. At eighteen, Solomon was declared king of Israel, and began that career that won him world-wide fame. He was not more than twenty-three when the Queen of Sheba visited his court and confessed, "It was a true report that I heard in mine own land of thy acts and of thy wisdom. Howbeit I believed not the words until I came and mine eyes had seen it; and behold the half was not told me."

In the history of the divided kingdom after the death of Solomon, it is singular that in not a single instance is the age of a king of Israel given at the time of his coming to the throne, whilst in the kingdom of Judah the ages of all her nineteen kings but two are given. Of the seventeen whose ages are mentioned, all are young men but one, Rehoboam, who ascended the throne at forty-one. Joash became king at seven years of age; Josiah at eight; Azariah at sixteen; Jehoiakin at eighteen; Ahaz at twenty. At sixteen Josiah began to seek the Lord; at twenty he began to purge Judah of idolatry, and at twenty-six repaired the temple. Hezekiah was only twenty-five when he restored the Temple of the Lord and destroyed the brazen serpent of the wilderness. For four hundred years Judah was ruled by her young men, and was captured and Jerusalem destroyed under Zedekiah at twenty-one years of age.

Any one who has read the history of Rome and Greece with care, knows the prominent part their young men filled in their national affairs. They were the athletes in their games and the gladiators in their contests; they occupied positions of prominence in their religious processions; they made up the mass of the scholars in their gardens and academies, and of the soldiers in their armies. It was their brain and brawn that made Athens and Sparta what they were in their prime, and it was the decadence of their moral principle that brought Corinth and Rome to what they were in the era of their decline. Alexander the Great was regent of his father's kingdom at nineteen; at twenty sat on the throne of Macedon, and while yet a youth won his victories and his fame, and at thirty-two died in a drunken debauch. Mark Antony was not thirty when he distinguished himself in Egypt and Syria. At twenty-three Julius Cæsar had made his mark as an orator before the Roman Senate, and at twenty-seven was chosen military tribune. Nero was but fourteen years old when he came to the Roman throne; and was twenty-seven when, first having set fire to the city, he sat on top of a tower, and, as he watche' the flames, "amused himself with chanting to his own lyre verses on the destruction of Troy."

The greatest event in human annals was the begir.

ning of the Christian era; yet right in its dawn stands John the Baptist, a young man of thirty years, and rings in the new era with his " Repent, for the kingdom of heaven is at hand ! "

Christ himself was a young man, thirty years old at His baptism, and thirty-three at His death. And the probability is that all His apostles were young like Himself. The fact that He foresaw the long journeys they would have to make and the severe hardships they would be called on to endure, would likely lead Him to choose as His messengers only those in the prime of early manhood. Of John, His beloved disciple, history states that he died A. D. 100, aged ninety-four. This would place his birth at A. D. 6. As Jesus was born four years before the year 1 of the Christian era, this would make John ten years younger than the Saviour, and so only twenty years old at his call as an apostle. His brother James was probably somewhat older, but not likely over twenty-five.

That the great Apostle Paul was a young man at his conversion, is evident from Acts vii.. 58, where in the martyrdom of Stephen, it is said, " The witnesses laid down their clothes at a young man's feet whose name was Saul."

At twenty-seven years of age, Charlemagne was master of the whole of Gaul and of Germany.

Charles V. of Germany ascended the throne of Spain at sixteen; took the government of affairs into his own hands, and at once became the most powerful ruler in Europe. At twenty he was crowned Emperor of Germany at Aix-la-Chapelle, and at twenty-five fought the important battle of Pavia.

Charles XII. of Sweden was a king at fifteen; beat the Russian armies before Narva at eighteen, and at twenty-five was on his way to Moscow, with the repute of being the greatest general of his age.

Louis XIV. of France became heir to the throne at five years of age; at thirteen declared himself of age and assumed the royal authority; at fifteen put an end to

the wars of the Fronde; at eighteen became his own
Prime Minister, and by his twenty-first year made his
court the center of literature, science and art.

Napoleon I. was a Brigadier-General at twenty-five;
at twenty-seven was at the head of the army of Italy;
before he was twenty-eight had beaten four· Austrian
armies, and at thirty-three was proclaimed Consul of
France for life.

General Lafayette was not twenty years old when
the American Congress accepted his service in the war
of the Revolution, and made him a Major-General in the
U. S. Army; and he was but twenty-seven when, at the
invitation of Washington, he revisited this country, and
made his memorable tour of the leading cities of the new
Republic.

John Calvin, whom Bancroft calls " the guide of
Republics," was already a thorn in the side of the Sor-
bonne at Paris, at twenty. At twenty-three his sermons
were publicly burnt in the streets of the capital, and at
twenty-six he issued his " Institutes," which at once
made him famous throughout Europe.

Martin Luther at twenty-four was Professor of
Philosophy at Wittenberg; at twenty-seven heard the
inward voice, "The just shall live by Faith," while on
his knees ascending the *Scala Santa* opposite the
Church of St. John Lateran at Rome; and was only
thirty-four when he inaugurated the Reformation by
tacking his ninety-five theses on the doors of the Schloss-
kirche at Wittenberg.

Have I not cited enough to show·that in the past,
the hand of the young man has been on the Helm of
Human Destiny? And who that knows anything of
our country and our era does not see the same youthful
hand at the helm to-day?

Individuals among our young men of the present
century may not rise to the unusual distinction possessed by many in the past, but the masses of them
enter into the movements of the day, and are giving
shape to human affairs as they have never done in any

previous age of the world. At home, and in commercial and political affairs, they are at the top of the tree. They rise the highest in our cares and solicitations. They are our chief pride and hope. This world seems made for them and not for our daughters. Fairy hands take them up at their very birth, and Fortune, the genial goddess, showers her gifts on them from the very cradle. The Goshen spots of home are assigned them; in their education and culture everything is done for them. Parents spend years in personal self-sacrifice, that their boys may be grandly fitted for life. When they step out into the world, helping hands meet them everywhere if they are worthy. Their life and energy and hopefulness are at a premium. In point of numbers, they throng wherever you turn. Our country seems to be a hive of young men. The census of 1880 reports for our whole land a male population of twenty-five and a half millions, and the one-fourth of that number are young men from eighteen to thirty years of age. Young men between these ages form one-sixth of the entire population of our thriving cities, and those from twenty-one to thirty-one almost half of our voting population.

It has been estimated that there are one million five hundred thousand men employed in the railroad business of the United States, a very large majority of whom are young men.

There are two hundred and fifty thousand commercial travelers making their tours over the land, sixty per cent. of whom are young men. A recent memorial to the Interstate Commerce Committee, from members of the amusement associations, states that there are five hundred organizations of circuses, theatrical and minstrel troupes and the like, in our country, and that, in one form or another, seventy-five thousand persons are in their employ. And who that is acquainted with these combinations does not know that young men make up their rank and file. Forepaugh's circus for the summer of 1887, employed about five hundred men, and when one of the officials was asked how many of them were young men, he replied, "All of them, and we take none under twenty-one years old."

These seven million young men of our present day are to be the future husbands of our daughters, and fathers of our children. They are to bring into being twenty million of our coming population before they die. If, as Goethe said, "the destiny of any nation, at any given time, depends on the opinions of the young men who are under twenty-five years of age," these young men are to shape our politics, give color to our education and character to this mighty Republic.

If all this be true, then I make a statement of momentous interest when I say that in our young men, American society is *dying* at the top.

CHAPTER II.

DYING.

The national committee of the Young Men's Christian Association has sent out a printed statement, in which I find that but five per cent. of the young men throughout the land are members of church; that only fifteen out of every one hundred attend religious services with any regularity, and that seventy-five out of one hundred never attend church at all. That is, putting the number of young men at about one-eighth of the population, of the seven millions in the United States, over five millions of them are never, or practically never, inside a Christian church.

Is this too low an estimate? Let us see. I have always heard it said of Pittsburg, Penn., that it is a community of worshippers. The church property of that city and Allegheny is valued at nearly six million dollars. Ever since the place was founded, religious work of the most solid kind has been carried on. Yet to-day, among the two hundred and eighty-seven thousand people who live in Pittsburg and Allegheny, and among the fifty thousand of their young men, only four thousand five hundred are found in all the churches, Protestant and Jewish.

New Albany, Ind., where I live, is a city of churches. It has been in the hands of Christian people for more than half a century. The place in that time has grown from a village to a city of twenty-five thousand inhabitants. Everywhere you meet with churches. The Methodists have, in all, seven places of worship; the Presbyterians have three; the Christian, two; the Baptist, two; the Episcopalian, one; Lutheran, one. In all sixteen houses of worship. They are all self-supporting and doing a grand work for Christ. At present there is in the city scarcely a family of any prominence that is not identified with some Christian church. Nearly one-third of the adult population over fifteen years of age, is in the membership of the Protestant churches. At the same rate of growth, these Protestant churches should have by this time over one thousand of the thirty-five hundred young men of New Albany. Instead of that number, they had, a few months ago, by actual count, in eleven of the twelve white churches, three hundred and twenty-five In all the Protestant churches there are not over three hundred and fifty young men on their rolls. That is, of every three young men the Church should have had, she has retained one and the world has gotten two.

The people of Springfield, Ohio, claim for their busy city a population of at least thirty-six thousand. Judging from the census of 1880, the males from the ages of eighteen to thirty comprise a little over one-sixth of the entire population. This would give Springfield about six thousand five hundred young men. By a count made in January of this year (1889) there were in the membership of the nine leading churches, four hundred and sixty-one young men of the above mentioned ages. These

nine churches include almost the whole membership of
all the protestant faith in that city.   Dr. Helwig, who
is now candidate for governor on the prohibition ticket
in Ohio, told me that in his judgment there are not over
five hundred young men in all the protestant churches of
Springfield. This means that of every one hundred young
men nearly ninety-three are out of the church.   Of the
five hundred, not one hundred and fifty take any part in
the work of the churches to which they belong.

The Young Men's Christian Association *Watchman*
of September, 1888, contained the following item : " There
are four hundred and twenty-five thousand males in Massachusetts and Rhode Island between the ages of fifteen
and forty, and it is safe to say that not more than one-
sixth of the number are members of evangelical churches."

Under the auspices of the Young Men's Christian
Association, a canvass was made among the churches of
Evansville, Ind., taking the limits as to age at sixteen
and thirty-five.   The footing up showed eight hundred
and sixty-five of the sixty-five hundred young men as
belonging to the evangelical churches.   " The estimate
includes a large number of probationers of the Methodist and Evangelical Lutheran denominations."

I. E. Brown, State Secretary of the Illinois Young
Men's Christian Association, writes : " In a city of ten
thousand inhabitants, whose statistics have recently been
secured, it is found that less than three hundred men are
in all the evangelical churches, and of these less than one
hundred and twenty-five are between the ages of sixteen
and forty."

In a valuable communication to me, Geo. W. Cobb,
R. R. Secretary at present, of the Young Men's Christian
Association at St. Louis, says : " I find in my own work
that the number of young men who profess to believe
in Ingersoll and spiritualism and materialism, and are
sceptics, is appalling.   It has been estimated that there
are from sixteen thousand to eighteen thousand young
men in Indianapolis, and that five to seven per cent. of

them are church members, and that fifteen to seventeen per cent. attend church regularly."

Mr. Cobb also furnished the following: "In one city of nineteen thousand population, were three thousand five hundred young men, and eighty-five were members of Protestant churches; in another of twenty thousand, three thousand five hundred are young men, and twenty-nine were members; in another of twenty thousand, four thousand young men, and thirty-eight joined in one year; in another of seventeen thousand, three thousand young men, three hundred and fifty were church members; in another of thirty-eight thousand, six thousand young men, and three hundred attended church; in another of thirty-two thousand, five thousand young men, and one hundred and five received into twenty-one churches during the year." These, says Mr. Cobb, are from carefully collected statistics, and are "cold facts."

It is not claimed for the above cities that they represent the best sections of the country. They are given to show that taking the land throughout, it is not putting the per cent. too low to say that only five young men in every hundred profess Christ. Desiring the names of the above mentioned cities, I wrote Mr. Cobb, and received in reply:

"Dear Brother:—I am unable to give you the names of the cities mentioned; they are facts, however, obtained from carefully gleaned statistics, kept by our State and International Committees. In moving from Indianapolis I lost books and papers, and those referred to are among them. It is a fact that some of our pastors refuse to accept such statistics. I myself, in comparing notes with two or three others, visited and counted the number of young men visiting the saloons in Madison, Ind., one Saturday evening, and also ascertained the number at church the next Sunday, and found that our calculations were true. More young men were found in two or three saloons than in all the churches combined. I found the same condition of things in

Atlanta, Ga., when stopping there, and if that Virginia pastor could stop in St. Louis a short time, he would be convinced that our figures do not lie. It is appalling, the number of young men and boys arrested for crime in this city. A boy not more than nine years old set fire to my barn last week, and it was nearly burnt down.

Yours sincerely,   Geo. W. COBB."

Rev. J. E. Gilbert, D.D., in an address on "Our Young Men," delivered at the Indiana State Sunday School Convention, June 22, 1887, asks with reference to the young men of Indiana:

" 1. Are they, in any considerable number, members of the church, of any church? The answer must be in the negative. In this state there are in round numbers four hundred and fifty thousand communicants in all ecclesiastical bodies. By a series of observations, carefully conducted, it has been estimated that not more than six per cent. of the whole number are males between fifteen and twenty-five years. That gives in the entire state twenty-seven thousand inside, and two hundred and twenty-three thousand outside. That is, ninety per cent. of all the class under consideration have not so much as entered their names upon the roll of any church whatever. Ten per cent. only have openly signified their purpose to be religious. These facts are the more startling when it is remembered that all are of an age to understand the nature and claims of religion, and that they are more susceptible to its influences now than they ever will be at any subsequent period of their lives. This test will enable us to judge to what extent religion will be a controlling element in coming manhood, and also how much of that manhood will be saved and enlisted in the cause of Christ. Here is the most exact measurement of the church for the next quarter of a century.

" 2. Are the young men attending our Sabbath-schools? According to the carefully prepared report of the Secretary of our State Sunday School Union, there were last year three hundred and seventy thousand, in round numbers, enrolled in the various Sunday schools of the state. As his figures were, for the most part, obtained from the published records of the various denominational bodies, they may be accepted as nearly correct; if, in any degree, they are not accurate, they exceed rather than fall below the actual numbers.

"For several years each Methodist pastor in the United States was required to report at Conference the number of pupils in his school fifteen years old and upward; and it was found, taking the years together, that these were about one-fifth of the entire enrollment. Reckoning on that basis, there are in the Sunday schools of our state probably seventy-five thousand persons over fifteen years. Making no allowance for the large number over twenty-five years, and assuming that the young gentlemen in Sunday school are as numerous as the young ladies, an assumption not warranted by facts, we have as a large estimate for the young men and older youth, from fifteen to twenty-five, attending Sunday school in Indiana, say thirty-eight thousand. That leaves two hundred and twelve thousand young men outside of the Sunday-school. How many of these find their way, even irregularly, to the services of the sanctuary on the Lord's day, no one can tell. But it is safe to say that not more than forty thousand hear preaching without attending Sunday school. That would leave still about one hundred and seventy thousand entirely, or nearly, beyond the influence of the church. In other words, the appointed agencies of religion are reaching probably not more than one-third, certainly not one-half, of the young men of our state.

"3. Another fact is closely related to the foregoing. There are in the state one hundred and twenty-five thousand boys between the ages of five and ten years. In the state of Maryland, by a thorough system of canvassing, it is found that eighty-five per cent. of boys of that age are in Sunday-school. Assuming that the same proportion holds in this state, it follows that of the one hundred and seventy thousand now wholly beyond the influence of the church and Sunday-school, all but about thirty-five thousand were once in our classes, receiving more or less religious instruction. In other words, the church at one time or another has had in its hands two hundred and twelve thousand out of the quarter million of young men; it has led twenty-seven thousand into nominal discipleship; it has retained a greater or less hold upon fifty thousand more, while one hundred and thirty-five thousand, or sixty-three per cent. of all committed to its care, have not only failed to accept the gospel, but have even refused longer to attend the place where it is preached and taught."

All of these statistics are gathered from our older states, and from sections where young men have not only had the opportunity of church worship, but where the most of them have, at least in early life, been brought in contact with religious services. There are places in our land where church privileges are exceedingly limited, and where the proportion of young men who lead a Christian life must dwindle to almost nothing. Mr. Burford, Assistant State Secretary of the Wisconsin Young Men's Christian Association, says of the Gogebic iron range, that at the beginning of the year (1887), "there are not less than ten thousand young men scattered along the trend of the ore deposit and in the vicinity of the mines. The above number is likely to be doubled during the summer." Whilst the Christian church has few, if any, places of worship for these young men, yet "the devil has two hundred sets of rooms open to damn the fellows, with a staff of about one thousand paid agents and many volunteers, and money in abundance."

Says Rev. W. F. Crafts: "I have discovered in this state (New York) a city of fifty thousand inhabitants—the majority of them being English-speaking—where there has not been an English-speaking Protestant church for twelve years, the only church having German service. I have discovered also fifty cities of ten thousand each, in this state, which have but two Protestant churches each, many of these being very small and feebly manned for lack of funds." These cities that Mr. Crafts has discovered, are down-town wards in New York City, in all of which there is said to be but one church for every two thousand and eighty-one inhabitants.

At the first Convention of Christian Workers held in Chicago, June, 1886, Rev. J. W. Weddell gave statistics showing the population of each of the wards in Chicago, and the number of churches in each ward. One ward of thirty thousand had but one church; another of forty-one thousand had but three churches; another of thirty thousand had but five churches. In Dr. Strong's book, " Our Country," it is stated that one of the districts of Chicago has a population of fifty thousand, with twenty thousand children under twenty years of age, and that in this district there is Sabbath-school accommodation for only two thousand, whilst two hundred and sixty-one saloons and dago shops are open night and day for their ruin.

Dr. Strong also quotes Dr. Dorchester as saying that though the evangelical church membership in the country at large numbered in 1880 one in every five of the population of the United States, yet in Colorado it numbered but one in twenty; in Montana, one in thirty-six; in Nevada, one in forty-six; in Wyoming, one in eighty-one; in Utah, one in two hundred and twenty-four; in New Mexico, one in six hundred and fifty-seven, and in Arizona, one in six hundred and eighty-five.

From such statistics as the above, which might be multiplied indefinitely, it is plain that the estimate which allows five young men out of every hundred for membership in the church is not too low. Indeed, it is exceedingly doubtful whether the proportion is that large.

To the above discouraging statements must be added this other, that of the young men who are in the communion of the church, not more than one-half of

them can be relied on for anything like active service in
evangelical work.   The churches over the country that
have their young men neither in the prayer-meeting nor
Sabbath school are legion.   Their consecration to the
Sabbath base-ball games is greater than to the communion of the Lord's Supper.

The pastors of a certain city were asked the questions, How many young men have you in your membership between eighteen and thirty years of age? and how
many of these are active workers in the church?   The
replies of eleven of them footed up three hundred and
twenty-five in membership, and less than one-half of
them in any active work.   The above city has a population of more than twenty thousand; yet Forepaugh's
circus, that exhibited in it in August of 1887, had three
times as many young men consecrated to its amusements
as have all the churches of that city in the ranks of their
active workers.   Said the Assistant Secretary of the
Young Men's Christian Association in a city of two
hundred thousand population: "We have four hundred
and fifty-two active and associate members in our Association, yet we cannot muster ten consecrated workers
out of them all."

Here, then, we have seventy-five out of every hundred young men in this country who do not attend
church; ninety-five out of every hundred do not belong
to church, and at least ninety-seven out of every hundred
who are carrying no cross and bearing no burden for the
redeeming of the world to Christ and His church.

In short, the young man of our day is substantially
figured out as a factor in Christian evangelization, and
were the whole population to come to his standard, the
church would almost be figured out as a factor in the
moulding influences of this great land.   From the Christian standpoint, this state of things is simply astounding,
and will stagger the most hopeful for a speedy evangelization of our country.   With only three of every hundred
of our own young men wearing the yoke for Christ, what

becomes of the prophecy that in one hundred years more the whole earth will have turned to the Cross?

It may be remarked that in most of the above estimates the Catholic church has not been mentioned, and the question be asked, Do you intend to exclude her young men from the ranks of the Christian army? By no means. When a young man is found consecrated to his Catholic worship, he is counted among Christians just as are those who are consecrated to Protestant service.

In the matter of statistics, estimates cannot be made among Catholics as among Protestants. The boys are all confirmed at an early age and are regarded as church members all through life, no matter what may be their characters, and the Catholic priests are reticent on the subject, so that nothing can be determined through them. But the same agencies that are at work to estrange Protestant young men from their church, are at work among those of Catholic homes. Owing to the fact that the adherents of Catholicism are largely foreigners, the tone of spirituality among its young men is lower than with the Protestants; hence the fact of such a large percentage of the convicts in our jails and penitentiaries being of Catholic persuasion. To an observer it is plain that the Catholic church has lost tens of thousands of her youth from her communion. Lapsed Catholics are found everywhere, especially among the men. They do not go over to Protestantism, but land in the world, where they retain the bias of their early education without its devoutness. It is no uncommon thing to meet young men of Catholic families who never attend any church, who utter no prayer and have never read the Scriptures. It is because Rome feels this hegira from her communion through the liberalizing influences of our country that the present system of separate Catholic schools is so rigidly enforced. It was an alarm measure growing out of the conviction that the whole fabric was in peril.

I asked a member of the Catholic church: Do your

young men attend your religious services? The reply
was, " No, they do not. In a few of our very pious homes
the boys are taken to church, and are often held there
till they are twenty-one years of age; but after that they
seldom come. Our priests are continually urging their
attendance just as you pastors do in the Protestant
churches."

As an evidence of the disintegrating influences at
work among Catholic boys and young men, I quote the
following from the *Catholic Home:*

" There is not a parish in Chicago where the Sunday
saloon has not been the ruin of hundreds of the most
promising and the brightest boys that made their first
communion in the parish church. There is not a parish
priest in this city but can furnish a long catalogue of
young men and married men whose loss of character, of
self-respect, of faith and virtue, whose downfall and prob-
able damnation, can be laid at the door of the open Sunday saloon. Is there any Catholic father or mother who
mourns the perversion of a son, any Catholic wife whose
husband abandons his home for the Sunday saloon, but
would rejoice to see these places of temptation closed?
Who are they that clamor for the open Sunday saloon?
Hard drinkers, inebriates, debauchees, and those who
minister to their vices, and grow rich on the misery of
wrecked lives."

What is true of the young men of Protestant and
Catholic homes is even more true among the Hebrews.
Time-honored Jadaism is fast losing its hold on young
men, and they are going almost *en masse* into infidelity.
Thus writes Mrs. Freshman, wife of the editor of *The
Hebrew Christian:* " The Jewish young men pay very
little attention to the religion of their fathers, though on
the day of atonement, the most solemn day of all the
year to them, they make it a point to be present in the
synagogue, but aside from this they are seldom found at
their services. They are drifting towards infidelity, and
if the Christian church were only alive to her duty, many
hundreds might be gathered into the fold of Christ."

There are those who think that the Jews are in some marvellous way preserved from the vicious influences that degrade and destroy in other circles. I have heard it stated from my childhood that there are no Jews in jail, and it is only a few weeks ago that, in this city, a celebrated Kentucky evangelist challenged an audience, " Did you ever hear of a Jew being in prison? No, sir, the Hebrews look better after their own than that." Had this evangelist studied the prison reports he would have found in the

Missouri Penitentiary, 1888	4	Jews.
Illinois Penitentiary, 1884	19	"
Ohio Penitentiary, 1888	4	"
Illinois Penitentiary, 1888	12	'
Tennessee Penitentiary, 1888	5	'
Elmira Reformatory, 1887	128	'
" " 1888	156	'
Cleveland Reformatory, 1888	8	'
Detroit House of Correction, 1888	3	'.

These facts are given only to show that no homes and no creeds are exempt from the blighting influences of the day.

The writer has no disposition to judge harshly those who are not in the membership of the church. He is well aware that many in it are not Christians — so is he certain that many out of it are Christ's own; yet these two things remain true, first, that it is poor personal religion that under favorable circumstances does not manifest itself in a public profession of faith in Jesus Christ ; second, that there is no Christian life where one is prayerless, and has respect for no kind of religious forms. If such passages as these furnish the basis of our future judgment —" Believe on the Lord Jesus Christ and thou shalt be saved," and " Whosoever doth not bear his cross and come after Me, cannot be My disciple,"— one of the terrible scenes of the great reckoning will be the arraigning of our seven million young men, and the terrible announcement to almost the whole mass of them, " I never knew you ! " " I never knew you ! "

CHAPTER III·

DEAD.

If our young men did no more than remain away from our churches, and would live under the control of moral principles, the case against them would not be so bad.   But the truth is that vast numbers of them are being lost to even morality.   They are dying at the top. All the elements that enter into ordinary manhood are being blighted within them.   Their story is one of lost purity and uprightness.   Their sensitiveness to truth, and home, and self has been blighted, and they are " dead in trespasses and in sin."   No one who has not given attention to it, dreams of the prominence of the young man in the criminalities and corruptions of the day.

It has been estimated that there are one hundred thousand tramps and vagrants in the United States who sustain themselves by begging from door to door. The vast majority of these are young men.   A sheriff, when asked what proportion of the tramps he fed during the winter months are young men, replied, " All of them."   A conductor spoke of the bands of vagrants he would often see from his train as he would be passing from city to city, as " camps of young men." After the murder of Jennie Bowman in Louisville, the first arrests were of tramps.   Six were taken up at one time, the oldest of whom was twenty-seven, and the youngest nineteen.

This last winter an organized band of tramps made their headquarters at the Coke Ovens, in Louisville. They soon became such a nuisance that the police determined to rid the city of their presence.   The plans were laid, and at eleven o'clock at night the rendezvous was surrounded, and not a single man escaped.

"Twenty-one tramps filled the patrol wagons. No tougher looking lot ever passed through the door of Central Station than this collection of professional loafers. In spite of their filthy faces and tattered clothes they seemed no objects of sympathy. Ranging in years from fifteen to thirty, they were one and all stout, able-bodied fellows, well able to support themselves if they were so inclined."

Our dead-beats, and swindlers, and shovers of counterfeit money; our gamblers, and rapists, and burglars, are mostly young men.

In August, 1887, at Salt Lake City, Fred Hopt was shot to death for murder, the laws of Utah Territory permitting the condemned a choice between hanging and shooting. "He sat with a cigar in his mouth, a rosette pinned over his heart as a target, and posing as if for a photograph while the firing squad of five aimed and fired." He was a young man.

L. I. Wilson, the letter thief of Kansas City, who punctured letters with a bodkin, and by a microscope examined the contents, was twenty-three years old.

Daniel Miller married a widow near Newport, Tenn. She had four children, a home, and two thousand dollars in bank. He persuaded his wife to sell out her home and go West with him. The homestead was disposed of, and with the proceeds, the two thousand dollars which had been in the bank, and four horses and a wagon, the young man, with his older but still blooming bride and her four children, started toward Chattanooga. When thirty miles from Newport, Miller stopped his wagon and picking up his wife and four children, threw them into the road, exclaiming:

"Now go back home, all of you, and be sure you get there —— quick."

Miller drove away rapidly, leaving his wife and step-children to get back home as best they could. Miller was twenty-two years old.

3

In August, near Macon, Ga., Thomas Wolfolk murdered his father, mother, their six children and a lady visitor in their home. The monster murdered them all by cutting their throats from ear to ear. Even the sucking babe lying sleeping in its cradle was not spared. Wolfolk is only twenty-seven years old.

In the same month, in Louisville Ky., an unprotected German girl had lost her bearings and in the dusk of the evening was hunting her way home when she was seized by a number of men, who were in the act of dragging her into a dark alley, when her cries attracted a policeman, who rescued her. The policeman described the ruffians as "six well-dressed young men," none of whom were "over twenty-one years of age."

The Turner gang of desperadoes living on Yellow Creek, Ky., was composed of ten men—all of whom, with the exception of Jack Turner himself, were young men ranging in years from seventeen to twenty-five.

It was young men who composed the majority of the band of roughs who kept Rowan county, Ky., for so long the scene of outlawry and bloodshed. A writer says: "Craig Tolliver was perhaps thirty-five years of age and the others younger, down to one of fourteen, who fought like a tiger."

John Thomas Ross, who was hung in Baltimore in September, 1887, murdered Mrs. Emily Brown to get fifteen dollars for her body at a medical institution. After breaking her skull with a hammer, he coolly tumbled her body on a wheelbarrow, trundled it through the streets to the college, and got his pay. He was twenty-six years old.

Albert Howell, the Boston letter carrier and thief, was a church member. While carrying on his criminal proceedings he would keep his Bible beside him in the office, and at every leisure moment could be seen intently reading it. His fellows would laugh at him for his piety, but he bore their scorn without a murmur. He was thirty years old.

One of the most fierce and bloody encounters that ever occurred between pugilists in this country, took place at Rocky Point, near Pawtucket, July 20, 1887. For over four hours, and in sixty-one rounds, Ike Weir and Johnny Havelin pounded each other amid the applause of the by-standers. Weir was twenty-nine years of age and Havelin but twenty. John L. Sullivan, who has done so much in this country to revive the barbarism of the old Roman pugilism and to brutalize the young men of the day, is not yet thirty years old.

The above instances are only a few of the ten thousand that are occurring every year. It is not the exception, it is the rule, that young men are the criminals of the day. From the single daily newspaper that comes into my home, the Louisville *Courier Journal*, I took down those cases of crime chronicled in seven weeks, beginning with May 1, 1887. Of the one hundred and eighty-two criminals, where the age was in one form or other mentioned, one hundred and sixty-five were young men. Of the fifty-three murders committed, all but eight of them were by young men. And nearly every one of the crimes committed by these one hundred and sixty-five young men was against the person, and in a form showing the basest instincts and lowest brutality.

If any are in doubt as to the prominence of the young men in the crimes of the day, let them go with me to our jails and penitentiaries.

Look into those faces, as regiment after regiment, brigade after brigade, division after division, passes by you in striped garb and with lock-step, and it is young men who return your gaze. Visit the camps of the Southern prisons, where convicts, as in Georgia, are subjected to the most brutal treatment, and where bloodhounds, as in Texas, are kept ready to pounce on the runaway, and whom do you see serving in a bondage tenfold worse than the most bitter servitude that ever fell to the lot of an old-time slave—but an army of young men?

Outside of the city of Philadelphia, on the route to Ocean Grove, the traveler sees to-day huge walls rising out of the ground. What are they for, he asks instinctively? They are too high for the foundations of great shops. They have no windows, and so cannot be designed for residences. They remind one of the great Chinese wall built to protect China against the inroads of the Tartars; and of the Cyclopean bulwarks within which the Babylonians took refuge from the attacks of the Persians. But these massive stone walls of Pennsylvania are rising not to keep foes out but to shut them in. They are for a new prison for Pennsylvania's increasing numbers of criminals, seventy per cent. of whom are young men and boys. Our own sons are the Tartars of to-day, and the walls that, throughout the country, incarcerate them, would, if placed end to end in a continuous line, rival in length China's fifteen-hundred-mile wonder.

In the following prison statistics, it will be remembered that the expression "young men" applies to convicts thirty years old and under:

	WHOLE NO.	YOUNG MEN.
Texas Penitentiaries at Rusk and Huntsville, according to Report of 1886	2,859	2,097
Joliet, Illinois, (1886)	1,494	971
South Carolina Prison received in two years, '85 and '86	547	391
San Quentin and Folsom, Cal., (1886)	1,891	886
Kentucky Prison received in 1884 and 1885	1,153	869
Ohio Prison received in 1886	812	502
Pennsylvania, Eastern, received in 1886	572	405
Pennsylvania, Western, received in 1886	265	179
Sing Sing, N. Y., (1886)	1,532	1,111
Auburn, N. Y., (1886)	1,084	639
Indiana, South, (1886)	525	358
Rhode Island (1885)	1,244	850
Connecticut, (1885)	276	153
West Virginia received in 1883 and 1884	205	152
Michigan Penitentiary received in forty-three years, up to 1882	7,281	4,886

To this list, published in the first issues of this work, the following may be added :

	WHOLE NO.	YOUNG MEN.
Indiana Prison, South, (1888) _____	539	372
Ohio Prison enrolled for 1888 _____	794	532
West Virginia committed in 1887____	97	66
Nevada received in 1888 _____	27	16
In Nevada Prison, Dec. 31, 1888_____	99	57
Indiana Prison, North, October 31, 1888_____	702	344
Georgia Prison, (1888)_____	1,537	1,421
Wisconsin, (1888)_____	438	224
Massachusetts Reformatory:		
1884-5_____ _____	663	469
1885-6._____	615	435
1886-7_____	662	441
1887-8_____	607	428
Vermont, (1887-8) .. _____	94	49
Connecticut, (1888) ____ _____	301	173
Reformatory at Ionia, Michigan, received from 1886 to 1888	1,378	945
Missouri received during 1887-8 ____	1,523	1,105
Rhode Island received since 1838____	1,397	953
New Jersey Prison, (1888)____ _____	881	494
Tennessee, (1889) _____	1,363 esti'd ⅞= 1,190	
Virginia (1888)_____	372	239
Illinois (Joliet) received from Oct., 1887, to Oct., 1888_____	650	436

From these figures we learn that, in round numbers, seventy per cent. of the convicts in our penitentiaries are young men. In the common jails throughout the country the per cent. is not quite so large, owing to two facts, that there is a larger per cent. of women among the criminals, and that there are often mere children, who, if they are sent up at all, are sent to houses of refuge, in the states where these refuges are provided. Still, even with both these classes counted in, the per cent. of young men is very large.

Frederick Howard Wines, in his " American Prisons," gives a table of the prison census of 1880, with the convicts numbered according to their ages. The whole number including penitentiaries, city and county jails, military prisons, and hospitals for insane convicts, is given as fifty-eight thousand six hundred and nine, thir-

ty-four thousand three hundred and eighty-five of whom
are young men from eighteen to thirty years of age.

Some people do not seem to be at all startled at
these statistics, about which there is no mistake nor fal-
sification.   They are met with, "Oh, young men are
naturally bad!" and "They are no worse than their
fathers!"   But they are our sons none the less; they
have immortal souls that are being lost; their criminalities are costing the government immense sums.   Society
has a responsibility with reference to these young men.
The mere fact that a boy is naturally bad, and that his
father was worse than he is, is no reason why we should
let him go to ruin without a desperate effort to save
him.   Is there nothing to stir men's souls in the fact that
every day of this year 1889, there has been heard, in the
penal institutions of what we call our "Christian cities,"
the tramp, tramp, of tens of thousands of young men?

There are few things about which the masses of our
people are more ignorant, than of the number and movements of our criminal population.   The almost universal
tendency is to under-estimate rather than over-estimate
the wide-spread extent of crime.   The more one looks
into the matter, the vaster grows the multitude, until
he stands appalled at the armies of criminals that file
before him.   It will startle many, the statement that one
in sixty of the present population of the United States
is either in prison or ought to be there.   Exact statistics cannot, of course, be given; but from the statistics
that are at hand, estimates may be made that will not
be far from the truth.

The most thorough and reliable prison report ever
made in this country, is that of Carroll D. Wright, U. S.
Commissioner of Labor, in his volume, "Convict Labor."
He gives sixty-four thousand three hundred and forty-
nine as the number who, in the penitentiaries, jails, and
reformatories of the United States, are engaged in convict labor; but he makes no attempt to enumerate the
convicts who are not so engaged.   In his catalogue are
only one hundred and fifteen jails, whereas there are in

the whole country two thousand six hundred and eighty-seven counties, each of which has its place for the confinement of prisoners. Apply to these counties the proportion, for instance, given for fifty-two counties in Alabama, and Mr. Wright's sixty-four thousand are increased to one hundred and thirteen thousand. That this number is too low, is evident from the fact that very few of the jails in our older and more thickly populated states are among those given by the commissioner. In the jails and houses of correction of only fourteen counties of Massachusetts, there are recorded four thousand convicts. In New York State, outside of its penitentiaries, there were last year, according to Wm. M. Round, of the Prison Association, twelve thousand five hundred and thirty-five convicts in penal institutions. This would make for New York's sixty counties an average each of over two hundred criminals, instead of nineteen, the average for Alabama.

Mr. Wright has no statistics at all from Delaware, Idaho, Montana, and Utah. The jails and lockups of New York City and the crowded criminal institutions of Blackwell Island are not in his list.

None of the city jails of such places as Philadelphia, Pittsburg, Buffalo, Cincinnati, Louisville, Chicago and St. Louis have a place in this report, because having no connection with the question of convict labor. It is placing figures inside the facts, rather than outside, to say that at any given time in the United States there are one hundred and fifty thousand convicts in its prisons, jails, and houses of refuge and correction.

Mr. Round, in "Our Criminals and Christianity," says: "By the best authorities it is reckoned that not more than one-fifth of the active criminals are in prison at one time." This would give our country a criminal population of seven hundred and fifty thousand, all of whom, within no great period of time, have actually been convicted of violations of law. So, say the same "best authorities," only about one-twelfth of all those whose living depends on crime, are ever convicted and punished.

Place the proportion as low as one-seventh, and, on the basis of the above estimates, we have a criminal population of over one million, or more than one for every sixty of our present population.   If this looks too large, remember that in the year ending September 30, 1886, there filed through the penal and reformatory institutions of Pennsylvania alone, an army of fifty-seven thousand seven hundred and seventeen, most of them arrested and confined for petty offenses, but criminals none the less.   Some of these may have been arrested more than once in the year, but not a large proportion of them.   Louisville, with a population of two hundred thousand, averages near eight thousand arrests a year, or one arrest for every twenty-five of its inhabitants; and Louisville is as orderly and law-abiding as any city of its size in the land.

Now apply to the above general estimates the proportion of seventy per cent. for young men; and subtracting one-tenth for female convicts, you have in prison at this date, in round numbers, ninety thousand young men, and five hundred thousand who are either now or have been convicted and incarcerated criminals—being one hundred and fifty thousand more than those young men who now make a profession of Christianity in the churches in this great land.

Three-fourths of these young men are native-born Americans and have had from childhood the opportunities of Christian civilization.   In the northern states seven-eighths of them have had more or less education, and cannot plead ignorance for their crimes; and a surprisingly large majority of them have had more or less of religious training.   Of the two hundred and sixty-two prisoners received into the Western Pennsylvania prison, only 5.34 per cent. had no religious belief.   Of three thousand eight hundred and sixty-two received into the work-house of Allegheny County, Pennsylvania, in 1886, all but one hundred and seven had had religious training.   Of six hundred and sixty-eight received in Joliet prison, Ill., in 1886, all but forty-three had attended Sabbath-school in the different churches. Of eight hundred and fifteen received in Sing Sing prison, six hundred and sixty-nine had attended Sunday school when boys. In four years ending September 30, 1881, there were admitted to the Michigan penitentiary one thousand one hundred and twenty convicts—six hundred and seventeen of whom came from homes where either one or both parents were pious.

This condition of things grows more dark and foreboding when we learn that crime in our country is increasing with greater rapidity than the population, and that it is having its largest increase from the youth of American homes. The prisons of the land are crowded beyond their capacity, and the cry to the legislatures everywhere is, we must have more cell-room. In the reformatories of the United States there are ten thousand boys, ranging from seven years to seventeen years of age, most of whom have been committed for the same crimes that are sending adults to the penitentiaries. Pennsylvania, for the year ending September 30, 1886, had more children in its House of Refuge and Reform School than it had convicts in both of its penitentiaries. Among the arrests by the police of New York City in 1886 were two thousand two hundred and forty-eight boys and one thousand and fifty girls, under fourteen years of age. In the Kentucky penitentiary, from January 1, 1880, to December 16, 1886, eight hundred and fifty-nine boys between the ages of sixteen and twenty years of age, were committed. Rev. W. W. Hill, chaplain of the California State Prison at San Quentin, states in his report for 1886: "During the last four years, notwithstanding the large percentage of discharges the number (of boys) present has increased from forty to eighty, or one hundred per cent. How much longer can we be indifferent to conclusions resulting from such facts? A few more one hundred per cent. increases and a new State prison must be built for the accommodation of juvenile criminals alone."

The biennial report of the Western Penitentiary of

Pennsylvania gives the "prison population" from 1826 to 1886. Taking the catalogue by decades, and with the exception of that from 1846 to 1856, the increase of convicts has been far beyond the increase of Pennsylvania's population for corresponding decades. The decade ending 1846 shows an increase of prisoners of seventy-one per cent. over that ending 1836. The decade ending 1866 shows sixty-one per cent. increase over that ending 1856. The decade ending 1876, shows eighty-one per cent. increase over that ending 1866; and that ending 1886, shows an increase of fifty-eight per cent. over the decade ending 1876. In all this sweep of sixty years, the very highest advance Pennsylvania has made in her population in any decade is thirty-three and one-third per cent.

The prison reports for 1873 showed a prison population throughout the country of eighteen thousand four hundred and ninety-two. According to the report of Carroll D. Wright, the same prisons in 1886 held thirty-three thousand six hundred and thirty-eight convicts, an increase of nearly eighty-two per cent.; whereas the whole population of the United States increased in the same period not forty per cent. In other words, so far as prison statistics afford a basis for judgment, crime in 1886 was more than twice as prevalent as it was only thirteen years before.

Wm. M. F. Round tells us in his "Our Criminals and Christianity," that from 1880 to 1886, whilst the population of New York State increased twenty per cent., that of her penal institutions increased thirty-three per cent.

Frederick H. Wines has an article in his paper of July, 1887, *The International Record*, on "The Increase of Crime." From statistics that he presents, crime is two and one-half times more prevalent in Pennsylvania than it was fifty years ago; in New Jersey, three times more prevalent; in Maine crime has advanced thirty-seven per cent. in twenty years. In Illinois the ratio of convictions is more than two and one-half times what it was thirty years ago. " In three states, Pennsylvania, New Jersey, and New Hampshire, the percentage of increase, above that of the general population, in fifty years, has been one hundred and fifty-two.

" In four states—including Illinois with those already named—the percentage of increase has been one hundred and four.

" In seven states—including Maine, Iowa and Minnesota—the percentage of increase for twenty years has been thirty-six. These seven states include nearly one-fourth of the total population, and it is fair to presume that there are more than one-third more convictions now in the entire country, in proportion to the population, than there were twenty years ago, at the close of the war."

The seventeenth Annual Report of the Allegheny County (Pa.) Work-house gives its population from 1870 to 1886. The number sent into it from Pittsburg alone in 1870, was eight hundred and fifty-three; the number sent in 1886 was two thousand, eight hundred and seventy-eight, an increase in sixteen years of two hundred and thirty-six per cent. If the general population of that city had kept pace in its increase with the increase of its criminals, Pittsburg to-day would have a population of over two million souls, instead of two hundred and eighty-seven thousand for both Pittsburg and Allegheny. Says General Brinkerhoff of Ohio: "So startling is the increase of crime, that it is very evident that society itself is in jeopardy, unless something is done to arrest and reverse this order of growth. According to the United States census, crime has more than doubled every ten years for half a century past, and still the tide is rising. It is evident something must be done, or we die."

The foregoing statistics are part of our country's census, as much so as those given relating to our crops, or mines, or colleges, or churches. They demand the consideration of every lover of his country. Emerson

never spoke wiser words than these attributed to his
pen: "The true test of civilization is not the census, nor
the size of cities, nor the crops; no; *but the kind of men
the country turns out.*"

CHAPTER IV.

WASTE.

Young man, I have just passed my fiftieth birthday.
So far as I know there is not a broken organ in my
body. If it were not for indications outside of my
person, in my grown children and in the records of the
old family Bible, I would not know that I was over
twenty-five years old. I cannot find at any point a
single trace of the wear and tear of half a century. Yet
have I gone under the billows of the severest bereave-
ment; have had vexations and trials all through my
public life, and have had bodily afflictions that would
have sent me to the grave if I had ever been dissipated
in any form.

These bodies God has given us for the first dwelling-
place of the soul are magnificent creations. They can
stand almost any strain upon them, provided it comes
in harmony with their laws. They are made to bear us
and serve us for one hundred years, and then to let our
souls out at the grave with the ease and peace of one
alighting from the chariot of a king.

But the draft you are making on your body, young
man, is the waste of dissipation. Because of your sinful excesses, the doom of the wicked will fall on you, and
you will not live out half your days. At fifty, as I turn
to look back, I find that I have nearly outlived the second generation of fast young men. Those of my boyhood days, who had as good bodies as my own, but who

subjected them to the drain of indulged passions, have been in their graves for fifteen and twenty years.   Many who were born in the beginning of my ministry, and "sowed their wild oats," are already dead, and those who remain are broken and diseased, dragging out the end of their short careers in misery.

Any one who studies carefully the mortuary lists will find a critical period of human life at infancy.   In the vital statistics of Ohio for 1885, one-sixth of the deaths fall within the first and second year.   The proportion of deaths gradually diminishes till we come to the columns from twenty to twenty-five years, and from twenty-five to thirty, when there is a sudden rise in the number. We all understand the secret of so great mortality at infancy. It is owing to the risks of birth and the exposure of babyhood.   But why should we reach another critical period at about the twenty-fifth year?   At that period the body should be at the beginning of its manhood prime.

Theorizers have imagined that human life has a kind of wave motion, unseen and inexplicable, yet real.   We come into life at birth in the trough of the wave.   At about three years of age the billow begins to rise, and remains at its crest till about twenty, when it begins to sink, till at twenty-five the greatest depression is again reached.   Then comes another swell that does not have its corresponding descent till fifty.

Practical people have no difficulty in accounting for these upward and downward movements of the mortuary lines.   At about fifteen years of age young girls fall into the foolish customs of society, and expose their health by only half dressing themselves.   They " catch cold"; important organs are disturbed; in many instances rapid decline follows and between twenty and twenty-five comes death.   It is only the wave-motion of exposure.

At the same age young men begin to have what they call "fun."   Their dissipation makes heavy drafts on the kidneys and lungs; digestion is broken, and the

heart's action enfeebled.   The twenty-fifth year comes
round, and a wasted manhood sinks into an early grave.

Young man, you are not ignorant; you know what I
say is true—that the sinking of your chances after twenty
is through your early vices.

Miss Willard quotes Quetelet, the famous statis-
tician, as having made a special study of the statistics of
European life insurance companies, and that he had
reached the conclusion that the time of greatest risk (or
highest death rate), in men's lives is the age of *twenty-
five years.*   She adds very wisely: " Unhappily the reason is not far to seek.   Indulgence in tobacco, alcoholics,
and impurity, if begun in early life, at the age of twenty-
five will have reported themselves back in the wretched
sequels of deterioration, often even unto death."

The following extract is from a physician whose
name I cannot give.   But the words are too true to be
omitted at this point.

"It is a sad but unavoidable reflection that thousands
of men who should be the bone and sinew of the country,
pillars of society, of the church and of the State, are
broken down, both physically and mentally, before they
have reached the zenith of their usefulness.   Early indiscretions, the results of ignorance and folly; over-exertion
of both mind and body, induced by inordinate ambition,
dissipation and exposure, are continually working the
ruin of thousands whose ability, energy and integrity the
world needs to preserve the equilibrium of civilization.
Some fall before they have yet entered the arena of
active life, while many more, enervated by the effects of
youthful folly, after a few years of ambitious labor, find
themselves incompetent for the arduous duties of business and professional life, and are forced to retire igno-
miniously from the field of action to meet an untimely
death, or to drag out a weary and unsatisfactory existence, incapacitated for both the duties and enjoyments
of life.   In the capacity of physicians it is our duty to
ignore all false delicacy and speak plainly on this subject, that the young may have due warning to shun

unnatural practices that lead to the subversion of manhood and the loss of everything that makes life desirable.
Let us also warn the unhappy victims of follies that are
past undoing to improve the means of restoration while
there is still hope. The reality is beyond adequate
description. In its track we find the ravages of loath-
some disease, physical, mental and moral degradation,
disrupted homes, asylums filled with imbeciles, and
graves that have kindly thrown the mantle of oblivion
over wasted lives."

What brings a blight on your body, brings a worse
blight on your immortal soul. You are in the slow but
sure process of exhausting all the higher elements of your
manhood. The tenderness of your affections; the keen-
ness of your sympathies; the kindliness of your ministrations; your sensitiveness against wrong; your respect
for the opinions and rights of others; your reverence for
truth; your devoutness toward your God, are oozing
away under these nights of revelry; and before you are
many years older, you will have undergone that awful
transformation that makes a brute of the man. A
brute! Why degrade an animal by comparing it with a
human being whose manhood is wasted. What animal
will take the life of its own kin? Will turn its own lair
or den into a hell of wretchedness? Will go howling
among the homes of its fellows, making itself a terror,
when it should be a support and defense? The Bible
stories of Cain killing his brother through jealousy; of
the sons of Jacob, selling Joseph into bondage out of
petty spite; of the sons of Eli robbing the people and
living in lust among the fallen women of the city; of
Absalom stealing the hearts of the people, and, under
cover of filial reverence and of godliness, leaving Jerusalem, to drive his father from his home, are sometimes
spoken of as the features of a barbarous era; but they
are being repeated all over our country to-day, by sons
who, in the indulgence of sinful passions, have turned
their hearts into stone.

In a city with whose homes I am familiar, I select a

section of thirteen squares in one direction and four in the
other, making a parallelogram of fifty-two blocks. In this
area within a single generation, I know of sixty young
men who have "gone to the bad." How many others
there may have been, in this section, among families with
which I am not acquainted, I do not know. But here
are sixty that I do know. Not one of them is from a poor
family, or that of foreigners. They are Americans and
from good homes. Most of them are from Christian
households, and have had an education both in the day
schools and Sabbath schools. Some have fallen through
drink; some through licentiousness; some are dead-beats;
some of them are tramps; some gamblers; some are dead
—dead either from self-violence or the violence of others.
The drain they have made on human hearts and human
homes, no one but God can know. The days of wretchedness to loved ones, and nights of painful anxious watching, will be revealed only when the books of the last day
are opened. One, after receiving his education for life,
marries a harlot, and is wasting his substance in riotous
living, and at the same time wasting the peace and sunshine of parental hearts. Another marries a young girl,
lives with her long enough to bring a child to her arms,
and then blights her life by running away with another
man's wife. A third marries a young girl who is supporting her home comfortably from her employment, and
takes her away from her income under promise of supporting her himself. In course of time a child comes to
their home, when he deserts her for another woman; and
to secure money to spend on his villainies, takes his
baby out of its cradle and sells the cradle. The poor
young mother loses a husband, sacrifices a lucrative position, and is left with a child in her arms to struggle alone
with the hardships of life, while the base scoundrel who
called himself her husband goes his way to turn the
sweetness of other lives into gall. So the whole dreadful roll could be called, every one as he marches through
his career of self-indulgence, trampling under his feet the
hearts of fathers and mothers and wives, and sending

their wails of bitterness before him to the presence of a
patient but just God.

The picture I have drawn is by no means exceptional. It is true of every town and city in this land.
All around, Davids are going up to the "chamber over
the gate," weeping and crying, "O my son Absalom!
My son, my son Absalom! Would God I had died for
thee, O Absalom, my son, my son!" Rachels are
mourning for their children and refusing to be comforted,
while you, young man, are having your "good times"
with your boon companions.

Rev. J. J. Talbot, who is mentioned in the following clipping from one of our dailies, acted as a supply at
one time in the Episcopal church of my own city. He
had the natural gifts to fit him for any position in life.
His career of dissipation had a very small beginning—
the sipping of the wine cup after communion. He was
never willingly a victim to his passion. At times he
would shut himself up for days that he might overcome
the awful thirst for intoxicants, but the demon within
him conquered him at last, and he died under its spell.
The following extract is given because it shows, in words
of pitiful pathos, the waste of dissipation ·

The Drink Demon.—J. J. Talbot, once a minister
of the gospel, then a brilliant lawyer and member of
Congress, lately died at South Bend, Ind., from the
effects of strong drink. Mr. Colfax heard him speak in
the following strain shortly before his death :

"But now that the struggle is over, I can survey the
field and measure the losses. I had position high and
holy. This demon tore from around me the robes of my
sacred office, and sent me forth churchless and godless, a
very hissing by-word among men. Afterward I had
business, large and lucrative, and my voice in all large
courts was heard pleading for justice, mercy and the
right. But the dust gathered on my un-open books, and
no footfall crossed the threshold of the drunkard's office.
I had money ample for all necessities, but it took wings
and went to feed the coffers of the devils which possessed

me. I had a home adorned with all that wealth and the most exquisite taste could suggest. The devil crossed its threshold and the light faded from its chambers; the fire went out on the holiest of altars, and, leading me through its portals, despair walked forth with her, and sorrow and anguish lingered within. I had children, beautiful to me, at least, as a dream of the morning, and they had so entwined themselves around their father's heart that, no matter where it might wander, it ever came back to them on the bright wings of a father's underlying love. This destroyer took their hands in his and led them away. I had a wife whose charms of mind and person were such that to see her was to remember, and to know her was to love. For thirteen years we walked the rugged path of life together, rejoicing in its sunshine and sorrowing in its shade. This infernal monster couldn't spare me even this. I had a mother, who for long, long years had not left her chair, a victim of suffering and disease, and her choicest delight was the reflection that the lessons which she had taught at her knee had taken root in the heart of her youngest born, and that he was useful to his fellows and an honor to her who bore him. But the thunderbolt reached even there, and there it did its most cruel work. Ah! me; never a word of reproach from her lips—only a tender caress; only a shadow of a great and unspoken grief gathered over the dear old face; only a trembling hand laid more lovingly on my head; only a closer clinging to the cross; only a more piteous appeal to heaven if her cup at last were not full. And while her boy raved in his wild delirium two thousand miles away, the pitying angels pushed the golden gates ajar, and the mother of the drunkard entered into rest.

"And thus I stand; a clergyman without a cure; a barrister without brief or business; a father without a child; a husband without a wife; a son without a parent; a man with scarcely a friend; a soul without a hope—all swallowed up in the maelstrom of drink."

This destructive work of yours, young man, does not end with yourself and your home. Your loss of personal honor and integrity sends you into the world as a dangerous element. You are to enter into positions of responsibility only to betray the confidences placed in you. You are educating yourself to become an absconding clerk, a defaulting treasurer; to draw on the funds of others to meet your own losses in reckless speculations; to unite with bands of others like yourself to "beat" your employers out of their honest gains; to become a "boomer" and rob the innocent through fictitious values placed on bonds and stocks and real estate; to enter some city council, or jury room, or legislature, and there squander the public funds to meet the demands of your godless ambition; to go to the polls in public elections to sell your own vote and buy the votes of others, and so defraud communities out of their just decisions.

Good people are astounded to-day at the columns on columns in our newspapers, filled with the villainies of men who have occupied positions of responsibility. Indianapolis was startled in January last to learn that Joseph A. Moore—a trusted citizen and high member of the church—had robbed the Connecticut Life Insurance Company out of half a million dollars, and still more startled to learn that at his headquarters this robbery had been systematically carried on for ten years. At present, Louisiana is disturbed over the fraudulent issue of bonds to the extent of hundreds of thousands of dollars. The enormous plunderings of New York City and Brooklyn have become famous the world over. Through "jobs" the capital at Albany, New York, has already cost eighteen million dollars. Its ceiling was the work of downright rascality. *Harper's Weekly* says· "It will remind the spectator that the shrewdest people under the sun can scarcely hope to put up an honest public building."

"John C. Eno, who was a banker in New York City, and succeeded in stealing over four million dollars from

the Second National Bank, is living at present in Que-
bec, the ancient capital of Canada, in a beautiful house on
the St. Foye road, for which he paid seventy-five thousand dollars of his ill-gotten gains. He is living surrounded by his wife and family, and putting on a great
deal of style, as he has the entrée of the best society.
He is frequently seen at the receptions given by the Lieu-
tenant-Governor."

"Thomas Axworthy lives in Windsor temporarily.
His absence is enforced by reason of his having stolen
five hundred thousand dollars from the municipality of
Cleveland, Ohio, while acting as treasurer of the corporation.

" Henry Dilckman, who robbed an insurance company in St. Louis of seventy-five thousand dollars, is a
fellow-townsman of Axworthy."

Such extracts as these could be given by the score.

The *New York Sun* is responsible for the statement
that the stockholders of the great railroads running west
and south-west from New York have been swindled out
of forty million dollars. "By crooked manipulation and
adroit financiering the officers in power have played the
part of thieves, and with their aggrandizement depreciated
the value of stocks and wrecked the roads whose affairs
they were elected to supervise."   Charles Francis Adams,
an expert in railroad affairs, is quoted as saying that this
uneasy and unsatisfactory position of the railroad system
of the country is to be accounted for by " the covetous-
ness, want of good faith, and low moral tone of those in
whose hands the management of the railroad system
now is."

The career of Henry S. Ives, a young man not yet
thirty years old, is a romance of iniquity.   Through the
passion for wealth, public men gathered round him and
were enchanted with his financial genius.   Without one
dollar of his own, he came to be the wonder of Wall
Street.   *The Courier-Journal* says of him :

"The public considered him as a thief, but so long
as the law did not the matter was but a trifle.   In his

early attempt upon the road he had drawn in with him a man of recognized wealth and great honesty. When the thief was called into court, suspicion fell upon this man too, and the blow killed him. The unscrupulous broker immediately formed a plan to rob his estate, amounting to seven million dollars. He was detected and brought into court. This time he could not blind justice, and the whole tale of the life and crimes of this man, Henry S. Ives, is coming out. Forgery and perjury have been his most frequent instruments, and he has hesitated at nothing. He has stolen millions of dollars, and has proved himself one of the most daring freebooters of the age."

Chicago is scarcely out of its excitement over the daring of the Anarchists, till it is startled by the great conspiracy to murder Dr. Cronin. For bribery and lawlessness, this will stand unparalleled in the history of American courts.

"Luther Laflin Mills, who is one of the lawyers assisting the prosecution in the Cronin case, and who is not an alarmist by any means, said yesterday to a group of reporters: 'I weigh well the meaning of my words. I fully appreciate the delicacy of the position which I occupy, and I will say that in the history of criminal trials there has been no more unscrupulous, audacious or wicked attempt to interfere with the cause of justice than there has been in the Cronin case. It is appalling on account of its effrontery, its utter disregard of the law, and its defiance of every known code of honor, honesty and legality. There has been nothing like it in the history of this country. There has been no such crime attempted against American law in my recollection, nor do I find any such attempt to pervert justice in the reading of the history of my country.'"

Grave citizens are reading these things and saying under their breath, what does it all mean? Is there any man whom we can trust?

There is no mystery whatever in this condition of things. It is simply natural causes working out their

effects.   Men do not gather grapes of thorns nor figs of
thistles.   These public plunderers and plotters are not
all at present young men; but they were once young
men.   In early life their moral characters became
vitiated, and robbery has become second nature to them.
And, if something is not done to elevate and christianize
the conscience of the present rising generation of boys
and young men, the future will be as the present, full of
the wrongs which one portion of society commits against
the other; our property will become less safe from the
threats of the anarchist; our lives less secure from the
burglar and highwayman; our investments will be more
and more jeopardized by the speculator; our elections
will pass even more fully than to-day into the hands of
the briber and " boodler," and our whole administration
of justice become a by-word and a scorn to other
nations of the earth.   The mere fact that this is a free
country, and that it is the people who govern, will not
save us from the ruin that has come on earlier Republics.
Our private and public life, and both our legislation and
administration, must be based on righteousness, or we
fall.   And what prospect have we for a new heaven
and a new earth wherein dwelleth righteousness, so long
as the mass of our young men have no fear of God
before their eyes?

Dr. Washington Gladden, of Columbus, O., delivered an intensely interesting series of lectures this summer at Chautauqua, on some of the social and political
problems of the day.   His lecture on "Trusts" was a
most serious and convincing portrayal of the danger of
these immense combinations, unless they are carefully
watched and guarded by the people and their represent-
atives in our halls of legislation.   What he urged
above all things else for our safety was a higher order of
conscientiousness in our citizens.   After the lecture I
sent him a copy of "Dying at the Top" and asked him
the question, What prospect have we at present for a
higher standard of conscientiousness?   It was asked in
no captious spirit, but in all seriousness.   Given, the

young men of the hour — drifting from all forms of religious life, and toying with the serpent that tempts with forbidden fruits — and there is no prospect of a condition of things any better than we have at present. I have faith that a better day is before us, but it will come only by our changing the existing status among our young men.

Young man, I wish I could end the story of your waste right here. But I must take you where you have, now, little thought of ever possessing any influence for destruction. You look on death as the end-all of your reckless career, except as you may live to reap the fruits of your folly. You make two mistakes right here; you think that all the reaping time is in the other world and that the sowing time is wholly in this world. But observe carefully and you will conclude that reaping and sowing are never wholly separated in your life. The lassitude and pain that follow on the day after a night's debauch are in the harvest time. You are reaping the whirlwind the very instant you have sowed to the wind. There are reapings of remorse and despair that are reserved; but they are only the more remote results that come after patient nature and a long-suffering Heavenly Father have waited for you to repent and return. But you resist the warning of the immediate ingathering; by and by nature is exhausted, and the Spirit is grieved away, and then you are abandoned to the extreme consequences of your long course of sin, and learn that it is not a figure of speech where the Holy Scripture prophesies weeping and wailing and gnashing of teeth for the deeds done in the body. After death your career will not be substantially changed. Your soul will be out of the body, but not out of this world. In the transition, you are moved to a higher plane of power and influence by having your spirit set loose from the limitations of a material body. On that higher plane, if you should go up from a pure and righteous manhood in the earthly body, you would be in a position to multiply your good works for others and your

blessedness for yourself, by—shall I say a hundred-fold
or a thousand-fold?—by a "fold" as far above that of this
earth as is the spiritual above the material.   But you
choose to go up to that exalted plane from a debased and
debauched manhood.   As you go you carry with you
everything but your body—your memory, your passions,
your tastes, your propensities, your desires for unholy
gratification, your hate, your vindictiveness, and, out
there in that land of spirits, you go on with your work
just as you did here.   Can that be so?   How can it be
otherwise?   My dear boy, please point me to an agent
that stops its influence by any change of form, or even
changes the character of its influence.

The fuel in your grates is consumed, you say; but
that means only that the elements of it are set loose.
The water and the gases go off into the great world
outside, and the earthy matter to where it was in the
earth before the vital powers of plant-life took it up.
Not an element has lost its being nor a single property
it possessed.   Each takes its accustomed place in the
rounds of Nature's work, to be, and to do, till the end of
time, just what its Maker intended.   A power, be it vital
or spiritual, when once sent forth from the Creator's
brain, never halts and never dies.   You are a soul; your
body is only its primal form; in death you are no less a
soul.   A soul is God's highest form of influence; being
in the image of God, that influence is, in its nature,
divine; because divine, it is continuous and continual in
its ever-increasing sweep and power.   In the great
future, you will do wrong as you do here; you will break
hearts, and wreck fortunes, and trample hopes—on and
on and on—unless you stop right where you are, revolu-
tionize your conduct and return to the God whom you
have despised.   Satan and his associate devils were
once bright angels in Heaven; they fell from their holiness
as you have fallen.   Did they cease to wield an influence
to destroy?   Are they not now those very fallen souls
that are possessing men and gratifying their hate and

revenge by ruining what God intends shall be saved and exalted?

Now, halt, young man, and count the cost. For a sinful gratification you are filling your body with disease; preparing for an early death; corrupting your higher gifts; loading up your conscience with the recollections of hearts and homes broken and dishonored; of property wasted; of society disturbed; of law violated; of God and man despised and wronged. And you are making forced funereal marches to the doom of a wicked, wasted child of the everlasting Father.

CHAPTER V.

WORMS BENEATH THE BARK.

With the young men of American homes I am in profound sympathy. What I have written has come from a heart that loves them, and consents to reveal their waywardness, only because, by so doing, they may be saved. It is the very fewest of our youth who go astray from desire and design. The great mass of them think they can sin just a little and then "sober up" and "settle down," as many of their fathers have done. Many sin because they have never known anything else. A current that had its existence before they were born, has taken them up and carried them along on its easy yet resistless wave. Thousands of our criminals never designed to be criminal; they will tell you so when you gain their confidence. They are sinned against more than they are sinning.

As a class, our young men are a noble-hearted set of fellows. They are kind and polite and generous to a fault. The public is under an immense indebtedness to them. With what polish they wait on you at the counter, and the offices of telegraph, telephone and railroad. They answer your thousand questions without a murmur; they wait till you gratify your whims, and dismiss you with smiles. They give you directions and carry your packages, and help you on and off the cars as gently and carefully as the trained attendants of royalty.

Miss Jennie Smith, of Dayton, Ohio, when an invalid, traveling over the country in her wheel-cot found railroad men so uniformly kind and gentle that she is now devoting her life to preaching Christ among them. "When an invalid, traveling on a wheel-cot, so carefully cared for by them, and finding how hungry they were for sympathy in their isolated position, cut off as they were from the means of grace, her heart was drawn out to them with desires to help them spiritually." Yet these same railroad men are tempted and exposed as no set of men ever were; they have homes, but seldom see them; churches, but seldom are allowed to enter them. Day and night they are on the road in the service of others, exposed to weather and accident. Those whom they serve ride in the trains they guide and guard, without a word of kindness or sympathy for these brave fellows. Their ministrations are given without grudge, and received by the public without thanks.

· In the *Railroad Gazette*, published in New York, issue of April 26 last, is found this statement: "A calculation based upon accident returns in the reports of State commissioners indicates that every year some two thousand seven hundred able-bodied men are killed, and over twenty thousand injured in the discharge of their duties as employes of the railroads of this country."

A writer in the *Messenger of Peace*, speaking concerning the railroad men of Iowa, says:

"Our commissioner law has been in force for ten years. This law requires railroad companies to report casualties of every kind to the board. In these ten years there have been killed and injured in this state by the link and pin coupling and hand brake alone, two thousand four hundred and twenty-six strong, able-bodied men, and the great majority of them young men.

"When these reports from the railroads commenced we had about four thousand miles of road ; we now have a little over eight thousand. The report of the commissioners for 1888 shows three hundred and fifty-two killed and injured by these two causes alone in this state last year.

" We have in this nation now rising one hundred and fifty thousand miles of railroad. If the same death rate and injury hold all over the nation as in Iowa (and we have reason to believe it is greater) there are not less than six thousand six hundred of these young men ground to death under the cruel iron wheels, or caught between the cars and more or less crippled for life each year in this country.

" This is indeed a fearful statement, and one the general public will be slow to believe just because of its awfulness. Nevertheless it is too awfully true. I am under rather than over the true facts. Railroad experts tell me I should make my calculations on the number of engines in use, rather than on the miles of road in the state. There is good reason for this. Then again Iowa is a temperance state. Her railroad men are almost universally temperance men. Our trains are handled by sober men, but be that as it may, here are the astounding facts : Three hundred and fifty-two either killed or injured in the state of Iowa last year and on this most favorable calculation, six thousand six hundred in this nation by these two causes alone."

How can one read and reflect on these facts without feeling that here is a body of brave, knightly gentlemen who deserve our sympathies and ministrations.

When men of such material are found, out of the religious life, and often in ways of sin, one cannot but say to himself : Something is wrong. These erring men were not born just as they are. They are a result. If a tree withers before its time, injury has been done in some way. The law of cause and effect holds its place as truly in the realm of human thought and human conduct as it does in the material world. Remove the *causes* of vice, and vicious characters will disappear, as readily as will fevers and pests when sanitary measures become complete.   Says Dr. Maudsley: " It is certain that lunatics and criminals are as much manufactured articles as are steam-engines or calico-printing presses, only the process of organic manufacture is complex."

It is the purpose of this chapter to study this "process of organic manufacture," whereby our young men are turned away from the church into lives irreligious and often criminal.

The first step claiming our notice, is undoubtedly

HEREDITY.

A few months ago, in one of our American cities, there was executed a young man of twenty-five years of age. He had taken the life of a companion, in cold blood, and in his right mind.   He did not deny his crime nor attempt a defense.   He passed through his brief trial with perfect stolidity.   He sang, chatted, told jokes, ate and slept as though he were as happy as any man alive.   The announcement of his conviction and his sentence was received without the tremor of a nerve.   At the execution, he examined the scaffold and the rope as coolly as if they had been a work of art.   At his request, he put the noose round his own neck, adjusted it, and gave direction for them to spring the trap.   When he was dead, the general verdict of society was—" He was a brute, and hanging was too good for him."   For my purpose I will call him Gracey, and ask — Who and what made him a brute?

People of true and solid culture will not find fault when I say that Gracey began his earth-life in the body of his father, where that strange brain power—whose mystery no man can fathom—determined that the germ should be human and not something else.

The father was not a criminal, but he was a bad man none the less.   He had come from a long line of low-lived ancestry, and never had an opportunity to be any

different from his parents. All his constitutional instincts
and propensities were of the flesh. Alcohol and licentiousness had made him a victim of passion. On the
germ-life within him, he stamped his character as
distinctly as he ever had stamped the outlines of his
face in his photograph.

The mother had been a well-meaning girl, and had
worked honestly for her living till Gracey's father had
first ruined and then married her. Their wedlock
became a licensed indulgence, and the mother, in time
and by harsh treatment, grew as hardened and debased
as the father. In this mother's body, Gracey lay for
months, isolated from all outside influences. The
mother poured her life-blood into his veins, and her
thoughts and propensities into his soul. Here was an
ill-begotten germ developing in an ill-constructed soil.

When Gracey was born, he was white because his
parents made him white; he had human hands and eyes
and feet, for his parents had them before him, and he
had their characters—their tastes and passions—folded
up in his baby heart, ready to spring into life in the
coming development. Parentage settled the direction
of Gracey's career. Does any one doubt it? This is
Heredity, doubtless over-estimated by some, but vastly
under-estimated by most.

It is not true that birth *fixes* character and destiny.
Character, in this world, is seldom ever absolutely so
fixed that it may not be revolutionized.

Some Catholic Archbishop is credited with a very
foolish remark· "Give me the children of the land till
they are five years of age, and Protestants may have
them ever after." The idea is that by five years of age
he could so fix their characters that they would ever
after be Catholics at heart. But any child can be
revolutionized after childhood or in manhood. You
may make a civilized man out of the child of an Indian;
a Christian out of the son of an idolatrous Hottentot.
The transformation made by the gospel of Jesus Christ
in such men as John B. Gough, Jerry McCauley, and

Dick Weaver, of the cock-pits of London, are a standing
evidence that character is never absolutely fixed.

It is not claimed here that Heredity *fixes* character,
only that it gives a marked and decided *trend* to it; so
much so that any system of philanthropy that does not
take it into account can never redeem the world from vice.
It was a fundamental law of the creation that every
creature was to "bring forth of its kind." To this law
we owe diversities that always have existed and always
will exist. It is a law that is sovereign in the spirit as well
as in matter. It is as impossible for a child begotten of
lustful and vicious parents to begin its life unbiased
from lust and vice, as for a serpent's egg to bring forth
an eagle. The fact that many a child of a low-lived
parentage develops early into ways of purity and
Christian devotion, only proves that God has placed in
our hands another law that may overcome that of
heredity—the law of Environment.

The following statement was made some time since
in the *Popular Science Monthly* in illustration of the
"Inheritance of Deformities": "One of the most
singular of these is the case of Edward Lambert, whose
whole body, except the face, the palms of the hands
and the soles of the feet, was covered with a sort of
shell, consisting of horny excrescences. He was the
father of six children, all of whom presented the same
anomaly at the age of six weeks. The only one of
them who lived, transmitted the peculiarity to all of his
sons, and this transmission, passing from male to male,
persisted through five generations."

Junius Henri Brown states his belief in heredity thus:
"What the Rothschilds have been, they are still— men
possessed of rare genius for pecuniary planning, and for
bearing the largest and most difficult enterprises to successful issues. They *transmit* the properties, material
and mental, which they have inherited. Their blood
flows in kindred channels, generation after generation,
and every drop of it dances to the jingle of coin. From
foundation to turret they are built up and bulwarked

with cash. In due process of development, the future Rothschilds may become sacks of shining sovereigns."

To any one desiring to look more minutely into heredity as it bears on vice and crime, let me commend a work published by G. P. Putnam's Sons, New York, entitled "The Jukes." It was written by R. L. Dugdale, and is an honest attempt of the author to reveal to society a source of criminality that even philanthropy has ignored. In this work we find that in seven generations a single abandoned home bequeathed to the world twelve hundred descendants, a large majority of whom were idiots, imbeciles, drunkards, lunatics, paupers, prostitutes and criminals. Seven hundred and nine of the twelve hundred have been registered, and their history studied in Mr. Dugdale's work. He finds that, while harlotry in the community at large averages nearly two out of every hundred women, it was over twenty-nine times more frequent among the Juke women. In the line of Ada Juke, better known as "Margaret, the Mother of Criminals," it was found that crime among the men was thirty times greater than that in the community in general. Of the five hundred and thirty-five children born, nearly twenty-four per cent. were illegitimate. Among the women of this Juke family, the number of paupers was seven and a half times, and among the men nine times, greater than in the community at large. Among the sick and disabled of both sexes, nearly fifty-seven per cent. were paupers, one man, "through hereditary blindness, costing the town twenty-three years of out-door relief for two people, and a town-burial."

Summing up the crimes and pauperism of this single family, Mr. Dugdale estimates that in seventy-five years it cost the public over one million two hundred and fifty thousand dollars, " without reckoning the cash paid for whisky, or taking into account the entailment of pauperism and crime of the survivors in succeeding generations, and the incurable disease, idiocy and insanity growing out of this debauchery, and reaching farther than we can calculate.".

HOME.

Our little hero came into the world under an unlucky star. Neither father nor mother hailed his presence. He was received and treated as an intruder. The vengeance of an angry parentage fell on his head. The mother wished him dead, and did everything, by exposure and neglect, to kill him. But he was destined to live and suffer, and to make others suffer like himself. In his home life, extending to his twelfth year, Gracey saw nothing but confusion and violence; and heard nothing except what tended to change his heart into stone. He was turned out of doors in the cold; shut up in dark closets as a punishment; locked in the house and left alone for hours. He was kicked and beaten by a drunken father and angry mother, till he was compelled, like a savage, to turn on them with whatever weapons came to his hand. He learned to lie as his only success-ful weapon of defense; and to steal as, at times, his only means of support. His face bore the marks of perverted passion, and his soul was rank with those appetites that lay dormant in his birth. He grew shy and fearful, and looked on every human being as his foe. His only com-panionship was with the boys of the street whose lives were as bitter as his own, and together the only congen-ial pastime they found was in doing what aggravated and tormented others. Here was the childhood of what society afterwards calls "a brute," and yet not at a single point was he responsible.

It is the story of the home life of thousands of boys. The majority of our desperate and hardened criminals sprung from just such conditions. In the New York State Reformatory, at Elmira, record is made of the parentage and home surroundings of the inmates. Of three thousand one hundred and thirty-four, only two hundred and eighty came from good homes, while all of the balance sprang from homes indifferent or "positively bad." These records show also that the smallest per cent. of the inmates are set down as having "left home

previous to ten years of age "— only five in one hundred·
while fifty per cent. were from those who were " at home
up to the time of crime "— showing that a child's chances
are increased for a law-abiding life by being taken away
from bad home surroundings. The only remedy for
these vicious households is in that slow change that
takes place in the revolution of character. Until that is
secured the number of criminals whom others force into
crime will keep up. Mr. Dugdale expresses himself on
the prominence of the home influence in these words:

" The family is the fundamental type of social organ-
ization, and as we found it was necessary to take the
family in its successive generations as the proper basis
for a study of our subject, so have we found, in those
cases where the established order of society has sponta-
neously produced amended lives, that the family hearth
has formed an essential point of departure."

It is not among the vicious classes alone that home
delinquencies have proved ruinous to boyhood and early
manhood. Many Christian parents mourn the lapsing
of their children from purity and uprightness, little
dreaming that their own omissions are the responsible
agents. Boys, especially, come in contact with an impure world early in life. They are thrown into its atmosphere in their early associations and at the public
schools. Secret habits are taught them, that from the
very beginning give their lives a trend toward what the
Scriptures call the "flesh." In these secret indulgences,
or rather abuses, is laid the egg that hatches out the
criminal, and produces a manhood in which all spirituality seems lost. The Master never uttered a truer word
than when He said, " Blessed are the pure in heart, for
they shall see God." .Thousands of our young men and
boys are not pure in heart. Their personal vices have
made them gross and vulgar in thought, and sermons
calling to a holy life leave no more impression on them
than on the cattle in the field. Boys enter into these
secret sins without knowing the wrong and danger of
them. They are taught them by their playmates, whom

they have not suspected of a design of injuring them, and they often never learn the blighting influence of them till, later in life, they find themselves the victims of a terrible vice. These boys have parents whom God gave them to shield them and rescue them from these beginnings of a low and sinful life, but who, from sheer recklessness or from a false sensitiveness, have left their children to learn of secret practices, not from those who would warn them against them, but from those who would teach them to practice them.

A factor in childhood that parents seldom take into account, is found in the sexual instincts. These are born in us, and belong to the Creator's plan in our formation. By His own provisions these instincts are made to develop early. Of all on the physical side of life, they are the most productive of good if they are guarded and controlled; but the most productive of evil if they are left alone. The average parent tries to conceal from himself and his child the existence of this sexual nature. The very terms by which its existence is designated are offensive to him. In his excessive modesty, this marvelous element in his child's nature never enters into his confidences and confidential counsels, and the child, with the possibilities of the second death in his body, is sent into the streets to learn the stuff of which he is made— and his parents go to their closets to mourn over their lost boy, and to wonder why their covenanted God will allow their child to be lost. It is not only on his physical side that a boy is neglected, even in church homes, but on his religious side; and in this lies one reason that so many of our young men seem to be wholly without serious religious convictions. It is a lesson Christian parents have yet to learn, that a Christian character is of slow growth, and comes like the growth of a tree, by silent but constant accretion. "Asking the Blessing" at the table three times a day; the singing of religious songs round the piano in the evenings; the reading of Scripture, and the offering of a prayer at the family altar twice every day, may appear trivial matters, but they make the atmosphere of home a religious atmosphere; and children, breathing it constantly, are unconsciously transformed into religious characters.

It is by keeping their children in daily contact with church forms, that Catholic priests do so much in the way of fixing their destiny for life. After their confirmation at twelve or thirteen years of age, these children may be turned loose into the world, but they go with a bias to Rome that dies wholly in but few, even of those who profess to be converted to Protestantism. As Protestantism has no priests, it is the parents of its homes that should give cast to their children's lives by a constant home devotion. But Protestant parents do not do it. Family worship is rapidly becoming a "Lost Art" in Protestant church households. The vast majority of them do no more than occasionally "say grace at the table," and thousands of them do not even do that. In a Presbyterian church which I served as pastor, finding that many of the young people who united with the church had no conscientious convictions in the matter of secret, and home, and public prayer, I felt that the reason of it must lie in the devotionless homes of the church. Taking a census of the congregation, I found but ten family altars among one hundred and twenty families. A Presbyterian pastor of more than thirty years' service in a single congregation, when asked how many of his families had family worship, replied, "Oh, not one in five." The Presbyterian discipline is very emphatic in urging the importance of home altars, and pastors, fifty years ago, made it part of their pastoral work to see that young married couples would begin their family life by reading and praying together; but of late years the matter has received less and less attention, until now, in hundreds of Presbyterian pulpits even, it is seldom mentioned. By consulting Moore's Digest, one can find scores of pages taken up in deliverances of the General Assembly on disputed doctrines, and in cases of discipline; but for eighty years there has not

been a single new, fresh, ringing deliverance on the
subject of worship in Presbyterian homes. What is
true of the homes of the Presbyterian church is true in
a greater degree in the Methodist, Baptist, Congrega-
tional and Episcopal households—devoutness of life in
the matter of religious worship is being turned over
more and more to a single day of the week, and to the
brief services of the sanctuary and Sabbath school.
According to the *New York Independent*, the church
population of this country is now nineteen millions.
From the United States census of 1880, we find that
there is about one family for every five of our population. This would give us for the country nearly four
millions of church homes. Out of these homes there
go every year into the world more than one hundred and
seventy-five thousand young men who have reached
twenty-one years of age. Allowing the high average
of one family altar to eight church homes, and we have
one hundred and fifty thousand young men, whom the
church ought to have in her active work, sent into the
world without having ever been brought into contact
with Christian devotion in the so-called religious homes
from which they have come. Such a condition of things
is simply shameful, when we consider the character of
the world into which our sons must go when they leave
home. The ancient Jew had better opportunities for
religious impressions. The two great principles on which
the Hebrews were redeemed from their corrupt condition
on leaving Egypt were, isolation from surrounding
idolatrous nations, and daily contact with religious forms.
Let any one read carefully the old Mosaic Ritual and he
will see that the children of Jewish homes never passed
a day without their eyes looking upon the sacrifices that
were offered before the Tabernacle. Let the same person
place the four million church homes of this country in a
row, and pass first through those that are practically
devotionless, and he will go through three million five
hundred thousand before he hears a single prayer
offered in a family group. Such a condition of things is

not even good Paganism. The old Romans had divinities called the Lares which they worshiped as the special providences that attended them everywhere. They were their domestic gods. It was the home hearth on which, as an altar, sacrifices were offered to them. "In all family repasts, the first thing done was to cast a portion of the viands into the fire that burned on the hearth, in honor of the Lares. In the form of marriage the bride always threw a piece of money on the hearth to the Lares of her family, and deposited another in the neighboring crossroads, in order to obtain admission into the home of her husband. Young persons, after their fifteenth year, consecrated to the Lares the bulla which they had worn from infancy. Soldiers, when their time of service was ended, dedicated to these powerful genii the arms with which they had fought the battles of their country. Captives and slaves restored to freedom, consecrated to the Lares the fetters from which they had just been freed. Before undertaking a journey or after a successful return, homage was paid to these deities, their protection was implored, or thanks were rendered for their guardian care." Thus it was that Roman youth were molded by constant contact with religious convictions and religious forms. Yet tens of thousands of Christian parents in this enlightened age expect their children to go into the world with finished Christian characters, after having spent their childhood and youth with no kind of home divinities or daily devotional forms.

A SECULARIZED SABBATH.

The only sun-spot in Gracey's life came a few months before his twelfth year. A lady for whom he had run errands persuaded him to join her Sabbath-school class. It was a revelation to the boy. He found himself in an atmosphere of kindness, and for the first time in his life gentle words were spoken to him. The sunshine fell into and began to warm his heart. In a few weeks the face did not look so harsh, nor the voice sound so rough.

Higher spirits were at work in the lad. It was the one
chance in his life. He was slowly yet probably surely
turning to the light like the vine that has sprouted and
groped in the darkness. But the sun-spot was lost and
with it went hope. Gracey found a place as chore boy at
the depot of his native place, where he ate and slept and
lived. The Sabbath was his busiest day, for it was then
the "cleaning up" was done. With the busy Sabbath
went the Sunday school, and the transforming angels
that would have redeemed this unfortunate child. From
the depot Gracey passed in time to the position of brake-
man on a freight train, where he remained toiling seven
days in every week till he committed his first crime
against the civil law.

I wonder if the busy people of this world ever dream
that a multitude are losing Hope through a broken Sabbath. Men may differ as to the Divine authority of the
fourth commandment, and with reference to the right of
the state to enforce its observance; but they cannot disagree as to the demoralizing influence of compelling seven
days of toil out of every week. Nature herself demands
the rest of the night and of one day in seven. It is a
physiological fact that when a man's body is kept constantly weary from unbroken toil, all the reviving ener-
gies of his nature are thrown into the nerves and muscles
to sustain physical exhaustion. He is compelled to live
simply a bodily life. The brain has no surplus blood for
thought, hence, as an organ of reflection, it shrivels. Why
is it that a tired man when he sits down at night after a
day of hard service, cannot read, but falls asleep over his
book? It is an exhausted body saying to the mind, I
have no strength left for you to do your work; I must
have sleep. Thus the mind is crowded out and the whole
man is materialized. This is true, not only of manual
labor, but of unbroken toil of any kind. The clerk whose
whole time for seven days in every week is spent in selling goods over the counter; the accountant who never
leaves his books but to lie down late at night to sleep;
the operator who hears nothing the year round but the

click of his instrument; the agent who knows nothing but to hand out the ticket and take in the price of it — all of them are in a tread-mill — that by its constant wear and tear is shortening their lives, and what is far worse, taking from them the time and restfulness they must have for the cultivation of their higher powers. The world is only beginning to see that the fourth commandment is founded on natural law as really as is digestion or the circulation of the blood. It says to every man, "You must rest one day in seven from your accustomed toil, or in your intellectual, domestic and religious, as well as in your physical interests, you must die."

Now, one of the appalling facts of our times is, that the only day in the week that God has designated for man's rest is being taken from us and forced into the service of the world. Our railroads, manufactories, telegraphs, street car and express companies, and many of our business establishments in all our cities, are compelling their employes to devote their entire seven days to their secular service. Christian people themselves are required to give up their only sacred day from their families and church devotions, or lose their places.

This secularizing of the Sabbath is telling most disastrously on our young men. They make up fully sixty per cent. of the employes on our railroads, and constitute the majority of all who live in the service of others. Their waking hours are all spent away from home influence, and the church has no opportunity to reach them with its regenerating agencies. Hence they are, from a social and religious standpoint, degenerating. They must degenerate until they are allowed proper rest from their exhausting toil.

A young man recently attended the evening service in the church of which I am pastor, and went to sleep. Afterward he apologized to a lady who shook hands with him, saying, " I could not help it; I was on the road all last night." And who could blame him? Two millions of young men in this country are out "on the road," in every-day service and almost all-night service, for men and for companies who work them like cattle. As a class, they are fearfully sinned against, and the blood of their loss will be demanded by a just God of those modern Pharaohs who force them into a bondage little less exacting than that required of the Hebrews in Egypt.

"Remember the Sabbath day, to keep it holy. Six days shalt thou labor, and do all thy work. But the seventh day is the Sabbath of the Lord thy God: in it thou shalt not do any work, thou nor thy son, nor thy daughter, nor thy manservant, nor thy maidservant, nor thy cattle, nor thy stranger that is within thy gates: For in six days the Lord made heaven and earth, the sea, and all that in them is, and rested the seventh day: wherefore the Lord blessed the Sabbath day, and hallowed it."

THE SALOON.

Gracey took his first lesson in saloon life in his father's home, before he was seven years of age. Frequently he was sent with the bucket for beer, when he thought it not wrong to help himself. The first money he earned was spent in the saloon. On one occasion, having taken more than his head could stand, the saloon-keeper made a bed of his coat under the counter, where the child lay till he "slept off his drunk."

When he began life on his own account, he had his evenings, as a usual thing, to himself. Where should he spend his leisure hours but at the saloon? Here were his companions. The room was bright and cheerful, and everybody was made welcome. A violin and piano helped to entertain all the comers. There was the daily newspaper on a rack by the fire, and here were games under the gas-light. No other place in the city was open for him—not a spot where he could feel free to spend an hour. The churches were open but one day in the week, and the homes were all closed to him. Of course he went to the saloon. Why should he not go? No one had ever taught him that there was any wrong in so doing.

Who can deny that the saloon has come in to meet a want? Young men without homes and young men with bad homes need a place of resort. Christian people were too slow in providing that resort, and the devil stepped in to meet the demand. "Will you walk into my parlor?" he said from his brilliantly lighted dens, and the young men walked in and were lost.

In the saloon Gracey *drank* what fired his blood and unsettled his brain; he *heard* the jokes and stories of the low and vile; he *saw* pictures that were lewd; and *read* the books and papers of the obscene and the anarchist. And here it was he learned to be lewd and licentious; for the saloon had its second story, where the lust of the fallen heart was fully gratified. So go thousands like Gracey, who do not mean to be lost, but are carried on by companionship and appetite till they enter the rapids, when all power of self-control is lost, and then comes the precipice.

Without considering the saloon in connection with American politics, its social influence is enough to condemn it forever. Saloon-keepers are not all bad men. Some of them are, in their German circles, men of standing and influence, and their saloons are quiet and orderly like themselves. They come to this country from Germany, where their business was respectable, and they have endeavored to keep it respectable here. I know some of these saloon-keepers who have raised families of sober and upright boys. But this better class is growing smaller and smaller.

As a class, saloon-keepers in our country are of the lowest characters. They are impure, profane, irreligious, vulgar and often criminal; and their saloons are like themselves. In no place, as here—outside of the bagnio—is the atmosphere so saturated with all that is vicious and corrupting. Here one meets with the world's filthiest characters, filthiest pictures, and filthiest conversation, because here congregate society's filthiest souls. The American saloon is the rendezvous of thieves, and cut-throats, and gamblers. Bummers, tramps, dead-beats,

throng around them as flies around the paper prepared
for their destruction.   Here it is, are planned our prize-
fights.   Here come the distributers of obscene literature
to ply their wretched traffic; here come the "boodlers"
to arrange for the corruption of our elections—here, in
these "Pest-Holes" of Infamy.   Yet it is a lamentable
fact that the principal patrons of the saloon are young
men.   Into a single saloon in Cincinnati, passed two
hundred and fifty-two men within an hour—two hundred
and thirty-six of whom were young men.   In New
Albany, Ind., in one hour and a half, on a certain evening,
one thousand one hundred and nine persons entered
nineteen of seventy-six saloons, nine hundred and eighty-
three of whom were young men and boys.   C. H.
Yatman stood on the streets of Newark, N. J., one day,
and in five minutes counted sixty-two young men going
into one saloon.   He passed his watch to a friend, and
asked him to stand and count for thirty minutes.   In
that time five hundred and ninety-two entered the saloon,
most of them being young men.   Yet this was only one
of hundreds of saloons in that city.   The two following
are from Richard Morse's " Young Men of our Cities":
"A city of seventeen thousand population, three thousand young men; one thousand and twenty-one, over
one-fourth, entered forty-nine saloons in one hour one
Saturday night";   "A city of thirty-eight thousand
population, six thousand young men; on a certain
Saturday evening ten per cent. of them visited seven of
the one hundred and twenty-eight saloons."

   In Milwaukee on a certain evening, four hundred and
sixty-eight persons entered a single saloon, nearly all of
whom were young men and boys.

   In Leadville, Col., on a certain Sabbath evening,
two hundred and fifty young men attended the eight
Protestant and Catholic churches; the same evening,
two thousand of the five thousand young men entered
six of the seventy-six saloons.   It is not surprising that
the church reports of 1886 showed twenty-five young
men admitted to the communion, and that the criminal

reports showed one thousand and ninety-seven arrests.

The following was clipped from the *New York Independent* of April 28, 1887:

"A sad story comes from Indianapolis of the discovery there of a gambling room for boys from twelve to twenty years old. The boys, employed as collectors, disappeared with funds, and this led to a search, which resulted in raiding a liquor saloon in a business block. Back of the bar was a room, at the end of which was what appeared to be a large ice-chest, but which was really a door leading to a room in the cellar, lighted with gas, in which were found forty boys, nearly all of highly respectable families, gambling at poker. They were smoking, and a number of them gave signs that they had been drinking. The police had been in utter ignorance of the place."

The Providence, R. I., Young Men's Christian Association furnishes the following:

On one Saturday evening, between the hours of eight and ten o'clock, by actual count, there were seen to enter two saloons within two doors of each other, respectively, twenty-six and twenty-eight young men in one hour and forty minutes. At another place, near the post-office, during the same time, sixty-five young men were seen to enter a single saloon. Still another saloon, within a few minutes' walk of the latter, ninety young men were seen to enter; at a fifth saloon, within easy walking distance of the largest number of boarding-houses in the city, were seen to enter within two hours, one hundred and forty-six young men. While the latter case is probably an exceptional one, it is believed upon good authority that not less than one hundred places are now open where an average of not less than fifty-two young men pass into these saloons every Saturday night, or an aggregate of over five thousand within the two hours. Upon the beat of a single policeman, eighteen places were found where liquors were sold to young men over the counter.

Evansville, Ind., has six thousand five hundred young men between sixteen and thirty-five years of age. There are twenty-six churches and two hundred and thirty-seven drinking places. By actual count, on a recent Saturday evening, four hundred and fifty-two young men were seen to enter four drinking places between the hours of nine and eleven. By actual count, there were only one hundred and forty-six young men in four of the representative Protestant churches in the city the next morning.

Springfield, Ohio, judging by the census of 1880, has at present not less than six thousand five hundred young men. At my own request statistics were taken last February with the following result: In the seven principal churches on a certain Sabbath morning were one hundred and seventy-one young men; in five of the leading saloons in one hour, the evening previous were six hundred young men. In that city are one hundred and forty-one saloons.

In New Carlisle, Pa., in December last, one thousand three hundred and fifty-eight young men entered eleven saloons from eight to eleven o'clock.

Mr. Meigs, of Indianapolis, Ind., delivered a lecture some time since in Terre Haute. Before his visit he had seven young men take notes for him in that city. The result was on a certain Saturday evening, that these young men found one thousand and forty-five young men enter seven of the one hundred and fifty saloons; and on the following Sabbath morning only seventy-five young men in all of the churches.

In Middletown, Ohio, there were taken for me the evening of Feb. 16, 1889, the following: In one saloon, fifty-seven young men in a single hour; in a second, twenty-seven; in a third, forty; in a fourth, sixty — one hundred and eighty-four in all. In the four leading churches the next morning there were ninety-seven young men present at worship.

The following comes to me from H. W. Kellogg, Secretary of the Young Men's Christian Association, at Appleton, Wis., dated Nov. 5, 1889:

"On Saturday evening, Oct. 26th, between seven **and** ten o'clock, there entered thirty-four of the fifty saloons of the city (population twelve thousand), seven hundred and twenty-five young men, two hundred and forty-five old men and ten women and girls — a total of nine hundred and eighty. Men under thirty were called young. During the same hours thirty-seven young men entered the rooms of the Young Men's Christian Association. Sunday morning, Oct. 27th, there were in six evangelical churches two hundred and eight old men and one hundred and eighty-four young men. Of this one hundred and eighty-four nearly one hundred were students whose attendance is required.

These figures are not as frightful as some in your book, but are bad enough for a quiet college town, as many think it. Very truly yours,

H. W. KELLOGG.

E. F. Hall, of Attleboro, Mass., writes October 30, 1889:

"While Assistant Secretary at Lowell, Mass., nearly a year ago, I visited nineteen liquor shops and carefully marked numbers and approximate ages from fifteen to forty years old. I was sadly surprised to find the result as follows: Number of places visited, nineteen; number found at each, smallest, eight; largest, forty-five; average, fifteen. Went to police station and found there were four hundred saloons in the city. Multiplying the number four hundred by average fifteen, we have six thousand young men in all these places during two hours' time, beside a large percentage going and coming. The population of Lowell is seventy-five thousand, making one in every twelve or thirteen inhabitants. I can hardly believe it, yet it is true. Rev. W. T. Perrin, pastor of a Methodist Episcopal church, accompanied me and stands a ready witness to this sad statement. Could give other experiences, but none more sad than **the** above."

In the *Association Dial* of Waltham, Mass., of October, appeared "An Eye Opener," which read:

"We have become very anxious of late to know where many of our young men spend their evenings, and that we might get an idea of the power of the saloon, we asked one of our members to station himself near the door of the saloon at the north end of the bridge, past which every person crossing the river has to go. By actual count, written on paper, we found, horrible to tell, that from 7 to 9 o'clock on Saturday evening, September 22, *three hundred and fifteen* men (most of them young men) entered the saloon, and in the same time *two hundred and twenty-six* came out.

"To show more forcibly just what these numbers mean, we give the total for every fifteen minutes: 7.00 to 7.15 o'clock, twenty-one; 7.15 to 7.30 o'clock, twenty-seven; 7.30 to 7.45 o'clock, thirty-five; 7.45 to 8.00 o'clock, forty-one; 8.00 to 8.15 o'clock, forty-six; 8.15 to 8.30 o'clock, forty-nine; 8.30 to 8.45 o'clock, forty-seven; 8.45 to 9.00 o'clock, forty-nine; total in two hours, three hundred and fifteen."

In the *Presbyterian*, of Philadelphia, of December 15, 1888, "Diogenes" published an article on "Wanted, a Young Man," in which he makes the statement:

"On a chief thoroughfare of the city I noticed a palatial building into which a constant stream of young men seemed to be passing. A gentleman informed me that, according to a careful count, four thousand men entered those ever-swinging doors on an ordinary day between six in the morning and ten at night. I thought in such a popular resort I might find the young man I was seeking. Entering, I passed by the bar into the large room beyond, where were two long rows of billiard-tables extending through to the back street. Around the first table alone I counted thirty-five young men watching the progress of the game. They were wasting their noon-hour. When I heard that it was not an unusual thing for merchants to walk through this place, to see whether any of their employes were there, I concluded the young man was not there that is 'wanted' in business circles.

"Joining some friends who wished to see who were to be found in the saloons about midnight, I made a round one night, and found that most of those we entered — some two hundred in all — were occupied by young men. But the young man that was 'wanted' did not seem to be among them."

From the report of H. J. McCoy—Secretary of the Young Men's Christian Association of San Francisco—for 1889, I clip the following statement:

"On Sunday evening, August 19, 1888, there were by actual count in all the evangelical churches of this city one thousand eight hundred and ninety-two young men between sixteen and thirty-five years of age.

" On the following Sunday evening, August 26th, the principal theatres, concert and billiard halls, and other places of amusement, including saloons, etc., were counted, (one base-ball match at which there were five thousand young men), and there were found in these places of amusement and saloons, including the base-ball match on the afternoon of that day, seventeen thousand nine hundred and thirty-three young men. And there were at least three thousand places of unhallowed influences which could not be reached and counted by our committee on that evening, where young men were congregated. Putting it at the very lowest estimate, we would say on that evening there were on an average five young men visited each of these places, which gives us a total of fifteen thousand. By these figures we find that there were at the least calculation thirty-two thousand nine hundred and thirty-three young men in the theatres, drinking saloons, and other places of amusement on that Sunday evening. This report is signed by ten young men, representing different denominations.

" The largest number of young men found in any one church was four hundred and eleven; the least, six.

" The largest number found in any one theatre was one thousand two hundred, and there were three places where there were over one thousand in each place."

Much more of this kind of material lies before me,

mind that it is the young men who are the principal
patrons of the saloon. They make up at least seventeen
out of every twenty. As there are not less than two
hundred thousand drinking places in this country, and as
twenty to each saloon is not a large annual allowance
from the ranks of our youth, I believe I am not overstat-
ing facts when I say that the saloon system of the United
States is degrading not less than four millions of young
men. What shall be done with the saloon as a place of
rendezvous is one of the grave problems of the hour. To
the writer it seems there is no solution but utter exter-
mination. Any other policy means the continuance of
the place of resort and of the sale of intoxicants. Reduc-
ing the number of saloons does not remove these objec-
tionable features. Indeed, what is gained by diminishing
the number is more than overcome by the concentration
of immense profits into a few hands, enabling them to
surround their ruinous traffic by the air of respectability
and the attractions of art. Parents feel that if every
saloon were transformed into a filthy and forbidding
shanty, the chances of saving their boys from the drink
curse would be immensely increased.

THE BAGNIO.

This search for the underlying influences that are
destroying our young men and boys would fall far short
of thoroughness if it overlooked that second story room
of the saloon.

Shall I, when I go to a physician to consult him with
reference to a cure, tell him all the minor symptoms of
my disease, and conceal the real disease itself? Many
do that very foolish and reckless thing, through modesty,
perhaps, and as modesty does not correct the trouble,
they wither and die.

Gracey in that upper room came under the most
blighting and corrupting spell of his unfortunate life. He

was just seventeen when he entered that dreadful **door,** that was to swing outward for him only when what little manhood was left in him was lost forever. Although he had not, up till his seventeenth year, been openly licentious, yet his whole career heretofore had prepared him for it, and when the opportunity came he yielded to it as naturally as the rain drops fall to the earth. The lustful impulse was in his blood; nothing had ever been done to restrain that impulse through an educated conscience. He had lived among people who had had no higher life than that of the flesh. Refined and Christian reader, you would have entered the same broad road to death that Gracey did, if you had had no better chance than he.

The fact is that a multitude of young men, who have been better born and bred, and who know better, are going into the hidden chamber of the harlot, and so are subjecting themselves to a blight, alongside of which intemperance is mild and gentle.

Between the time of his taking the first glass till he becomes a sot, the drinking man may long retain many of the finer elements of his manhood — his sincere attachment for his home, his self-respect, his sensitiveness of conscience — but lust degrades its victim at the very start. It corrupts life at its fountain-head. It is the canker of the soul, the rapid consumption of all that is distinctively manly and God-like.

It is a dreadful comment on the so-called modesty of the Christian world, that its magazines, newspapers, and pulpits have been almost wholly silent on the so-called social vices. Hush! hush! the refined have cried at every·public reference to them, till licentiousness has well-nigh undermined our social fabric. Its prevalence is truly appalling. The better classes have been ignorant of it, because it is a malady that moves in silence, and preys on its victims in the night-time and in concealment. It has no plain advertisements in the newspapers; pastes up no flaming posters; glows with no electric lights: is surrounded by no bands of music. It is this secrecy that **leaves** so many parents and reformers in ignorance, and, when the thin veil is lifted, makes them incredulous of what is revealed.

It is no intention of the writer to create unnecessary alarm in what follows. He is perfectly aware that many who are evil themselves, are prone to magnify the errors of others in order to excuse themselves; so is he aware of the fact that there is a large class of so-called physicians who, in order to sell their remedies, would make us believe that all of society is corrupt. There is no occasion for universal suspicion. Young women need not feel that every young man who approaches them is unclean. It is not true that all the diseases flesh is heir to are the result of lustful habits. Still, the social vices are fearfully prevalent. If one-half of what the witnesses state is true, the alarm should be sounded, and immediate steps be taken to check the progress of the plague. Lust begins its degrading work in the libidinous desires and visions of the heart, and in the practice of self-abuse among children. This unclean devil possesses far more than any one has dreamed of. There are honest physicians, like Dio Lewis, who declare it is almost universal, and that to these secret habits of self-pollution are traced the nervous disorders, broken constitutions and enfeebled intellect of tens of thousands of our youth. Said the Chicago *Inter-Ocean:* "Out of thirty-two young men in New York City who were recently examined for West Point cadetship, only nine were accepted as physically sound. Such a note might well make the young men of our cities pause for a moment's thought. Beer, the cigarette, too much amusement, and the *Hidden Vices* are making havoc with the physical manhood of all our towns and cities."

A statement comes from Detroit to the effect that during the last eighteen months an unusually large number of young men had been sent to the asylums in the state of Michigan. It was suspected that cigarettes had been the cause of the malady; but Health Officer Duffield, after examining various brands of cigarettes,

found no opium in them, and expressed it as his belief
that insaniiy was not caused by their use.

The following statement from a distinguished
physician probably will explain the cause: "Would I
could take them with me in my daily round (at Ham-
well Asylum) and point out to them the awful consequences (of self-abuse) which they do but little suspect
to be the result of its indulgence. I could show them
those gifted by nature with high talents, and fitted to
be an ornament and benefit to society, sunk into such a
state of physical and moral degradation as wrings the
heart to witness, and still preserving, with the last rem-
nant of a mind gradually sinking into fatuity, the
consciousness that their helpless wretchedness is the
just reward of their own misconduct." It was under this
consciousness of self-ruin that a young man exclaimed
" Medical men, who know about such things, and refuse
to speak out and warn the young against this vice,
ought to be killed, every one of them. Just a hint
from my father or the family doctor, or a little book,
would have saved me. The doctors, and the clergy,
and parents, and all the rest of them say, ' No ! keep still !
You must not say a word.' What in heaven's name are
doctors and parents for, if they can't give a single hint
to the young about such things? If I had a million
dollars I would give it all to spread information about
this horrid vice." Says Dio Lewis: "This species of
indulgence is well-nigh universal, and as it is the source
of all the other forms—the fountain from which the
external vices spring—I am surprised to find how little
has been said about it. I have looked over many volumes
upon sexual abuses, but do not recall a single earnest
discussion on this point. Believing that this incon-
tinence of the imagination works more mischief than
all other forms of evil—that, indeed, it gives rise to all
the rest—I am astonished that it has received so little
attention."

The extent to which the external form of licentiousness, known as the social evil, has become prevalent, is

awakening serious apprehensions for the future of
American society.   If prostitution undermined and
ruined Greece, and Egypt, and Rome, and Venice; if,
in a spiritual sense it has enervated the Latin races of
the Continent; our modern enterprise and our multitudes
of churches will not save us, if this same vice is allowed
to capture our youth.

A traveling man—an elder in the Presbyterian
church—when asked, "Do you find in your travels that
our young men practice to any great extent, the social
evil?" replied, "Oh, it is horrible!"   A physician of
good standing who was asked, "To what extent do our
young men violate the Seventh Commandment?" said,
"Ninety out of every hundred cohabit with women
before marriage."

Another physician when asked the same question
replied: "It would astonish you—not ten men out of
a hundred are guiltless."   Still another physician—a
member of the church and a praying man—said: "I
have practiced medicine in this county," naming it, "for
more than a quarter of a century, and I tell you not five
young men out of a hundred are pure."   Still another,
of unimpeached character and grown old in his practice,
said, "When I was a young man, not one woman in
twenty was solicited for her ruin; now I sometimes think
that not one in twenty escapes solicitation."

These statements are given, not on the supposition
that they are perfectly accurate, but because they are
the opinions of serious men who have opportunities of
knowing what they state.   There are communities
where the per cent. of pure young men is very much
greater than as given above.   Taking the country over,
perhaps it is stating too much to say that only one in ten
young men is free from the guilt of adultery.   The
very safest judges, in the presence of some great evil,
are likely to over-estimate its prevalence.   But when
sober, serious men make such statements as those above
given, the exact truth—if we could find it—must be
startling.   From all sides the testimony is uniform that

the young men of this day, *as a class*, are impure, and that licentiousness is rapidly on the increase.

The following is an extract from a letter written me by one of our State Young Men's Christian Association Secretaries. Its testimony is in the same line:

"A letter came a few years ago from a city now numbering eighteen thousand, in which the charge was made that in the middle and lower classes nine-tenths of the girls were ruined before marriage. Being in that city a few months afterward I mentioned the charge to a physician of large practice, with the remark that 'It could not be true.' 'I don't know,' said he; 'a friend of mine, a physician, has just told me that he *now* knows of *forty girls* who are soon to become mothers.'"

A railroad man having a large number of men in his employ, stated that every one of them visited bagnios. Said a gentleman to me: "I have twenty-five men under me, and only three of them refrain from intoxicating drinks." I asked how many of them refrain from sinning with women. After hesitating a moment he replied: "About as many." An Assistant Secretary of the Young Men's Christian Association, in one of our great cities, in speaking of the prevalence of the social vice among young men, said: "We have even found that some of our Yoke Fellow Band have been visiting these bad houses."

A letter comes from Jamestown, N. Y., saying: "Twenty-six young men entered one house of ill-fame in one hour on a recent evening in this city. A proprietress of one of these places is known to have stated recently that she took in two hundred and fifty dollars in one week."

I give the following from one of our Louisville dailies, because I know the truth of the statements. It is addressed to the ladies of the two fashionable streets of the city.

"Dear ladies, are you aware of the fact that some of you have sons of the tender ages of twelve to sixteen years, who, after visiting a place of harmless amusement, go to a popular eating-house and noisily partake of a midnight lunch, then enter a neighboring saloon (bar-room), and after an indulgence in beer, wine or whisky, resort to the purlieus of Green and Grayson streets? At 3 o'clock in the morning these scions of excellent families, having finished the night's carousal, return home and slip upstairs to bed. This is no fancy picture, and the scenes may be witnessed nearly every night. Mothers! take a peep into your boys' sleeping apartments occasionally and you may save a valuable life from wreck and ruin!"

From traveling men themselves comes the statement that young men "on the road" are greatly given to licentiousness. "Drummers," as a class, have a better reputation than they once had, for merchants have found that they cannot afford to employ men who are known to be corrupt—but thousands of them visit houses of ill-fame as regularly as they go to their meals. Worse, by far, than drummers, are the young men who travel with amusement troupes. They infest our streets after night; they deliberately lay their schemes for the ruin of girls foolish enough to be pleased with their attentions. How often they succeed, those in the ranks of abandoned women can best testify. Said a clergyman whose life-work is the rescuing of women from houses of ill-fame: "The most of the girls who resort to these houses in their shame, have been ruined by traveling men."

These facts thus far have come from the northern states. But when one turns his face southward, the same condition of things stares him in the face. Said a gentleman to me, "in all the region where I lived, there were only two young men—brothers—who were known to be absolutely pure, and they were looked on as something wonderful. People said they ought to be ministers."

Slavery, while it existed, degraded the negro women; but they remained women, none the less, and possessed all the attractions woman has for minds that are impure. Their degradation threw off the white men the restraint that social equality begets in the presence of white women; and negresses in the South, took the place of the houses of prostitution in the North. Thus it happens, that while the white men of the South degraded the negro women, they now, in their turn, are degrading the whites through their young men and boys. A clergyman, who was born in the South and knows its people well, said that twenty out of every hundred mulatto women are mistresses of white men and boys, and "society does not seem to care much for it." Said a gentleman who has traveled extensively in the South: "Many boys of fourteen years of age have their 'coons,' as they call their colored mistresses." A judge remarked to this same gentleman, "I have daughters and the young men of the city call on them; but I do not know but that, ten minutes before they call or ten minutes after, they have been in the embrace of negro women." A southern young man related to a business man, as coolly and indifferently as if it had been an item of trade, how he and certain companions had attended a " swell" party in the city where they lived, took home their girls after the gathering had broken up, and then spent the balance of the night with mulatto girls. And when asked whether that was a common thing among the young men of his city, replied, " Oh, yes, very common."

The following extract from a letter received from a Southern merchant, speaks for itself:

" My observation would lead me to say that boys as young as fourteen may be heard talking in their boasting way of their 'coons,' as they call them, and if half they claim is true, they may be found in bad houses kept by the dusky maidens as often as their elders. * * * I have heard good Christian young men say that they were actually seduced by their nurses or 'mammas,' as they call the darkies who take care of them from the cradle to an age of independence. * * * But the fault does not lie wholly with the nurse, for married men, I am sorry to say, raise whole families of these ' off whites' right on their premises, and you can hear small

boys speaking of this or that darkey as being the son
of some prominent man. * * * I regard the state
of morals found in the South as being one of the curses
of slavery, when each young man had his 'coon' on the
plantation and nothing was thought of it."

The extent of the social evil among men may be
learned from the number of women who are engaged in
it as a business.   Mr. Dugdale, who had large opportunities for judging, says in his "Jukes," that the number
of prostitutes in our cities is about 1.8 per cent. to the
hundred women, or eighteen in one thousand.   The
testimony of such authors as Dio Lewis and Kellogg is
that the "kept" mistresses far outnumber the prostitutes
of the bagnios.   It is not placing the average above the
estimates of competent judges to say that there are four
courtesans to every hundred women between the ages of
sixteen and forty—or one in twenty-five.

Some time since, in a lecture in Springfield, Ohio, I
stated that there were two hundred and sixteen women
of public ill-fame in Omaha, who paid a tax on their
prostitution.   When I was through, a student at the
Wittenberg Theological Seminary stated to me that, at
the Alliance that met in Omaha in 1888, the names of
four hundred of these women were given; and that, when
in that city recently, a gentleman who was in a position
to know told him that there were one thousand fallen
women in Omaha.   Putting the number at eight
hundred—twice that of the public women—and you
will have one fallen woman for every twenty-five women
between the ages of sixteen and forty.

The following from the *Daily Herald* of Omaha of
July 11, is pitiful, when you consider that "the Silent
Ones" are the daughters of American homes:

"A very handsome income indeed is the city's share
of the profits of prostitution in Omaha.   The sum
varies slightly each month, but one thousand five hundred
dollars is a low estimate of the average receipts per
month.   This month the amount bids fair to exceed this
figure, one thousand one hundred and seventy-three

dollars and fifty cents having been paid to the Clerk of the Court yesterday   All through the day, a silent procession wound its way to the Clerk's desk and another line of silent ones glided out.   If a child brought the money it was invariably a sable-skinned cherub. Trusted negro women, servants, and, in a few cases, the keepers of houses appeared in person.

"'Do we look upon this monthly tribute as upon a fine?'   One of the latter class repeated the question put to her, and replied: 'A fine—why should we? when to all intents and purposes it is a license, alike in all cases, with a large fee from us who run the houses?   The city and state laws would have the world believe us all criminals.   But we are not.   Oh, no; that couldn't be, because the city exacts a share of our receipts and so becomes our partner.   If confidence men, and burglars, and the like would do their work without fear of punishment they should make the city a partner.   I am opposed to the license because if our business can be made legal by a bit of hush money tendered the city every month, why then it is legal without that formality.   But it would be very impolite to refuse to pay the license.   The result would be like refusing to give the road to a locomotive.'"

Having seen in one of our periodicals the statement that there are ten thousand "public women" in San Francisco, I sent the clip to Robert S. Boyns, the Secretary of the Young Men's Christian Association of that city, and asked him with reference to the truth of it. From him comes the reply:

"As regards the number of public prostitutes in the city I will quote from a letter which I have just received from the Secretary of the California Society for the Suppression of Vice.   He says: 'Some two years ago I undertook a count of the houses given up, *notoriously only*, to prostitution in San Francisco, and the count also of women who are known as *public prostitutes*.   At that time I reckoned that there were eight hundred of that class, not including the Chinese.   It would not be surprising to me now if one thousand two hundred could be counted.'"

"Personally I consider this a very conservative estimate. There are four streets here *wholly* given up to houses for prostitutes, and parts of two others.

"The extent to which young men here visit these places is simply appalling. San Francisco is a regular home for quack doctors who do more to increase the vice than perhaps any other agency.

"It would be impossible to say how many young men here visit these places habitually. Certainly *thousands* do, and then there is a whole army of men who have what are called 'kept women.'"

Omaha and San Francisco are not exceptions to all our large cities. In the census of 1880, staid old Philadelphia confessed to five hundred and seventeen houses of ill-fame; Baltimore to three hundred, and New Orleans to three hundred and sixty-five. Any one can do his own figuring as to the proportion of the women employed in these houses. The census will show about one-fifth of the population of any city to be women from fifteen to forty years of age. Take Frederick H. Wines' average of five women to each bagnio, and then Dio Lewis' plan of doubling the public women to include all the loose women in a city. When this is done, he will be astonished at the army of the fallen that move nightly on behind the curtains of social life, thousands of them sent where they are by the falsity of the men whom they have trusted, and bewailing the fate forced on them for life, partly by people who worship very reverently at the altars of the forgiving Christ, without doing any forgiving themselves. I have said it publicly and say it again, some of these fallen women are better than many who are out of the bagnio, but who scorn the touch of the penitent sinner. Physicians tell me that from this doomed class come some of the most kind and tender of the nurses of the sick. Why do these better women not leave their degraded life, do you ask? Simply because, while there may be one fallen woman

in every twenty-five of their sex, there is not one woman
in twenty-five who would not cast a penitent off if she
were to wash her feet with tears and wipe them with
the hair of her head. Some good people ought to shiver
when they read—"Jesus saith unto them, verily I say
unto you that the publicans and *harlots* go into the
Kingdom of God before you."

But these ranks of fallen women must live; and
many are supported in magnificence by their prostitution.
By far the majority of their patrons are young men.
But in very large cities the heavy end of the expense is
paid by married men, who foot any bill rather than be
exposed.

Young men are always welcomed, but as a class
they have no great amount of money to spend, and so
cannot contribute the immense sums needed to meet
the outlays of the more fashionable places of resort.

One of the surprising discoveries in this investiga-
tion was found to be the relation of many physicians to
the licentiousness of our young men. Before me lies a
medical work, translated and recommended "as one of
sterling merit." One of the doctrines it proclaims is
that young men in the prime and vigor of their early
manhood must have indulgence for their passions, or
disease must result; and it goes so far as to explain to
them how they can visit houses of ill-fame and prevent
the contagion of the diseases usually prevailing there.
It says:—"Considering that there are many men in
large cities who do not get married, because they either
have not the means of supporting a family, or because
they do not find any one whom they desire to marry,
prostitutes seem to be a necessary evil for the time
being."

The writer, being anxious to learn to what extent
the Medical Schools and practitioners adopt such a
theory, has communicated with a number of reliable
physicians. The result has been a sad revelation of an
unseen and largely an unknown peril to our young men.
Many physicians hold to Gollmann's theory, and very

many more recommend to young men who have injured
themselves by self-abuse, that they resort to nature's
way of curing themselves, by visiting houses of ill-fame.

When I asked one physician, "Are there many
doctors who give young men such counsel?" he replied,
"Lots of them."

A physician in whom I have the greatest confidence,
sent me the following reply to some questions bearing
on this subject:

"Physicians disagree in their opinions as to the
necessity of sexual intercourse.

"Many believe it to be necessary to health. Others,
and among them some of the best, hold to the opposite
view. My opinion is that the first class are in the
majority.

"I know of no medical works of standing which
teach the doctrine in 'Gollmann's Diseases.'

"Medical works, however, are generally silent on this
subject.

"Medical Colleges, so far as I am informed, give no
such instruction. Medical students, as physicians, differ
in their opinions and go into the practice with such
differences."

The great defect in the medical science of the day
is that it is practically materialistic. The majority of
physicians are not only not Christians, but they do not
hold to any religious belief. Their practice requires their
attention seven days of the week; hence, as a class, they
are deprived of the evangelizing influences of contact
with religious forms and devotions. Many of them are
agnostic in their convictions, and practically blot out
God and immortality from their thoughts. With such
men, the human body is their god. To cure it of its
diseases is their glory; and they will cure it often irre-
spective of methods or morals.

He who advises the victim of self-pollution to secure
health by commerce with women, only counsels him to
escape one danger by plunging into a greater. He recommends a vice as a remedy for an abuse—a sin that damns

the soul for a disease that damns the body.   Better let a young man go to the asylum and die a raving maniac, than jeopardize his soul by indulgence in what is a thousand times worse than madness.   Indulgence with woman, outside of married life, is, under any circumstances, a violation of one of God's greatest commandments, and must incur a penalty proportionate to its greatness.   Christ would not even tolerate the looking **on a** woman to lust after her. He pronounced it adultery. The Scripture law of morality is that of continence. " This is the will of God," says Paul, " even your sanctification, that ye should abstain from fornication: that every one of you should know how to possess his vessel **in** sanctification and honor; not in the lust of concupiscence, even as the Gentiles which know not God, for God has not made us unto uncleanness, but into holiness." " Know ye not that your bodies are the members of Christ?   Shall I then take the members of Christ and make them the members of a harlot?   Flee fornication; **he** that commiteth fornication *sinneth against his own body.*"

Physicians who give this horrid counsel to young men, seem to forget that it involves the degradation of women.   No pure young woman would be willing **to** cure any young man from the results of his personal uncleanness, by sacrificing her virtue.   None but harlots **can** enter into the *materia medica* of these so-called physicians; and what is a harlot but an abandoned woman—lost to honor—lost to the world. Must young men be *cured* by the keeping of lost women, as doctors keep leeches, for sucking the blood? This whole doctrine is monstrous—it is leprous with the vileness of the infernal pit, and young men should shun it as they would shun " the worm that dieth not."

So do such physicians forget that in sending young **men** to houses of ill-fame, they are subjecting them **to** diseases vastly more blighting and loathesome than **any** **re**sult of the abuse of self.

Said a physician to me: "There is **no** such virulent

poison in nature as that which a fallen woman communicates to any one who touches her." Arsenic, strychnine, and other poisonous substances, are, in our drug stores, labelled with the skull and cross-bones, and placed on shelves from which they are not taken except under some physicians' prescriptions or on call of persons who are well known. Yet these poisons, when they enter the human body can be antidoted; and in time the system will eliminate every particle of them. But the poison to which a physician would subject a young man, in sending him to a bad house, has no antidote. When once in the body it is never thrown off; it lurks there, like a wild beast lying in wait for its prey, and may pounce on the body in which it lives at any moment. Said a gentleman, pointing to the splendid residences on Fifth Avenue, New York, " I would not for all these mansions have one drop of syphilitic poison in my blood." What is still worse, this dreadful poison goes from parent to child by inheritance, and from husband to wife by contact, until the home is filled with wretchedness. Yet with all this knowledge before them, and knowing that there is no certain means of preventing this poison being communicated from the courtesan to her male companion, there are physicians that would cure young men by exposing them to the horrors of the house of ill-repute. Knowing these things to be true, the very best medical works and medical professors are silent. They are continually instructing medical students as to the best methods of meeting the diseases of the body; but, every year, hundreds of these students are sent into the world, and into our families, with low ideas of personal virtue, and without a warning from book or professor against such unchristian and unchaste doctrines as that quoted from Gollmann. Let parents beware. Physicians should be selected for your children with the same care that you select teachers in your schools. To turn a boy over to some traveling doctor whom nobody knows, or to some home physician whose morals are known to be bad, is reckless.

The foregoing facts would not be presented here if the theory they involve had not become so wide spread. It has swept like a contagion among our young men, and thousands attempt to reason themselves into the belief of it, because it panders to their lusts. But it is an utter abomination; the tongue that proclaims it is "set on fire of hell," and the young man who commits himself to it, is doomed beyond hope. The very swine of our styes and dogs of our streets—with passions like our own—can survive and fatten in their continence. No physician dreams that indulgence is essential to their vitality. And why cannot young men, born better than brutes, preserve their health by a life of self control? The doctrine of continence is the doctrine of virtue; it is that of the medical schools of the day, and our high-toned physicians scorn the couclusion that the young man must be indulged. Nature makes no mistakes; she has provided profusely in all her secretions, but she knows how to dispose of all surplus without necessitating any creature to commit sin. Says Dio Lewis: "If a healthy man refrain entirely from sexual pleasure, Nature knows well what to do with those precious atoms. She finds use for them all in building up a keener brain and more vital and enduring nerves and muscles."

There are physicians who would scorn to give such counsel as has been mentioned; but who, when they find a young man abusing himself, will advise him to hunt up some nice virtuous young woman and marry her. The only difference between this counsel and the other is that it transfers licentiousness in many cases to the home, and prostitutes the marriage relation. What an exalted idea of wedlock! How flattered a young lady would feel if she knew some young man, in response to his physician's advice, had offered his hand to her to cure himself of a bad case of carnality. There is enough licentiousness carried on under the sanctity of wedlock already, without physicians making use of it as a healer for their corrupt young patients.

It is not absolutely necessary that men, diseased

from their depravity, should be cured nor that they should live. Better let them die than to expose woman-hood and childhood to their low propensities.

It is with great pleasure that I introduce here Dr. J. D. Buck, Dean of the Pulte Medical College at Cincinnati, and one of the best physicians and educators in the West. With his consent I give the following letter:

Rev. J. W. Clokey,
        My Dear Sir—

I have read your letter of 18th inst. and your pamphlet "Dying at the Top." You do not overstate the crime of the age that man commits against himself, and against the divinity within him. You diagnose the disease correctly, and my own experience for more than twenty-five years justifies all you say, and far more. But as to cause and remedy, pardon me if I say you must in my judgment go far deeper. If the "family altar" be indeed the halo of divine life, instead of a mere outward form, hurried through in order that the postulants may rush to "business," it will be indeed well. If the progenitors of "our boys" practice unrestrained licentiousness in wed-lock, the transmission of lust is as sure as though the prostitution were not sanctioned by "law." This disease, my brother, is deeper seated, ingrained, and is as surely transmitted, in spite of the family altar, as where nothing of the kind exists. You have touched the issue of all our diseases, but the remedy must be more than a palli-ative. Cut out the plague spot and the ulcer will not heal. The treatment must be constitutional and radical, and preventive as you say. Any doctor who recommends prostitution to cure masturbation is ready to *damn two souls to save one body*, and deserves to be hooted in his community. We need to move bodily to higher planes; young and old, male and female, in wedlock and out of wedlock. The religion of Christendom is a sham. The religion of Christ is an everlasting verity. I have written hurriedly because I must, but I take you to be dead in earnest, and if so, you will find the whole truth and the remedy. This truth will not dishonor Christ, or break down real Christianity, but honor the one and save the other.

Sincerely yours,

J. D. BUCK.

July 19, 1889.

In one of our court rooms sits a young man under the charge of murder. The crime has been committed under circumstances such that the jury can bring in but one verdict, and that is death.

The face of the prisoner must once have been an attractive one. The brow is full; the features are regular; the eye is bright, but from the face every expression of manhood is gone. It is a face one both fears and pities. Not a friend sits near him. An attorney appointed by the court pleads his case. But the prisoner is listless. He evidently has neither hope nor despair. All the finer elements of the human soul are dead in him, and he does not care what becomes of him. The " worms beneath the bark " have done their work, and there is not a green leaf nor fresh twig left. The law may kill his body, but others have already killed his soul. Not a nerve moves, not a feature is changed as the jury files in and reports its verdict of guilty of murder in the first degree.

Verdict! Verdict! Where is the jury that will bring a "verdict" against the father and mother, and saloon-keeper, and courtesan, and physician, and the society that have made this criminal what he is? It is Gracey. Poor fellow! the last that is seen of him is in the dissecting room of a medical college. He had bequeathed his body to the college. Before he is cut up and thrown into the vat, some students, young men like himself, prop up his nude body, place a silk hat on his head, arrange themselves around him with silk hats on their heads, and have their photographs taken. It is a fit closing to the farce called human brotherhood, in which an immortal soul comes into life in sin, passes through it in neglect, and goes out with a jest. What

God thinks of the whole procedure will be learned farther on.

"It must needs be that offences come, **but woe to** that man by whom the offence cometh."

CHAPTER VI.

HOPE.

Clouds, black and ominous, hang right over us in our national sky, and the heavens are full of angry mutterings; but above shines the sun, and its beams come flooding through the rifts in the darkness, telling us the day is not far away.   Clouds at best are only transient things and have never long resisted the glory and warmth streaming from beyond them.   The sun, not the storm-folds, is the king of earth, hence brightness is the daily promise for the future.   When one looks backward through the ages of human history he finds society at a hundred points in a vastly worse condition than it is in our country to-day.   It was worse in the England of one hundred and fifty years ago, when infidelity and social corruption were almost universal; but God sent the Wesleys to sound the alarm, and one of the greatest reformations of history was the result.

Europe in the Middle Ages was so fearfully corrupt that for awhile it looked as if there would never come a reaction.   But under Luther and Calvin and Knox society swung back toward God in that marvellous movement that gave us all the glory of our modern civilization.   At the close of the old era and at the coming of Christ, Paganism was supreme everywhere but in Judea, and Judaism had become degraded to Pharisee-ism; but under the preaching of John and Christ and the disciples, out of that chaos of ignorance and vice sprang the New Testament era, that in four hundred years brought a Christian King to the throne of the

Cæsars. In the days of Ahab in Israel, idolatry, on the surface of national life, had possession of everything; but, in the retreats of Judea, were seven thousand who had not bowed the knee to Baal. Individuals often become thoroughly depraved, but society never has and never will. God ever preserves a "seed" to do Him service, and that "seed" at every crisis' point has possessed sufficient numerical and spiritual power to throw back the tide of sin. It was society's latent godliness which, called into activity by the Elijahs and Johns and Wesleys, lifted mankind from idolatry to Christianity, destroyed Phariseeism, Paganism, the old-time Papacy and English Deism, at each victory exalting n ankind to a higher level from which it has never receded. The student of history cannot lose hope. The gradual rise of the Christian tide is unmistakable. Sometimes the waters have stood still, and even seemed to ebb far out from shore; but he who waited and trusted saw them come back again with a mightier power. This is the best era the world has ever known ; and this is the best decade of that era. Before us is still a better; beyond that a better; beyond that a better—one rising above another, like peak piercing above peak, till the heights of the future are lost from sight in the glory of the coming of the Son of Man.

The present diseased condition of American society is functional, not constitutional. We are in an era of marvellous progress. This progress has come upon us with such rapidity, that we have not had time to adjust ourselves to it. The wealth of the country has advanced with phenomenal strides. Money has never been so plentiful, nor so easy of possession; massive fortunes have been made in half a life time; the Goulds and Vanderbilts have accumulated more than the worth of many of the kingdoms of older times. American youth have been dazzled by these sudden splendors, and lost their balance in the pursuit of riches. The speculations of our country have proven maelstroms, in which thousands have been engulfed, not only financially but

morally.   By and by, taught in the school of bitter experience, we will settle back into the sober ways of slow
but sure accumulations, when our young men will become temperate in their aspirations, like the times in
which they live.

The inventive genius of modern times has thrown
new devices broadcast through our land as rapidly as
if they had come from the workshop of the gods.   New
machines, new weapons, new methods of communication
and transfer, spring hourly into form, as from the head
of Jove.   We are in an era of bewildering advancement,
and can scarcely find our bearing.   In the meantime
Vice is taking advantage of these improved methods,
and crime is increasing because of increased facilities.   It
speaks through the telephone.   It dispatches over our
telegraph wires.   It rides on our steam cars and steam
boats.   It makes use of our improved tools and ma-
chinery and we cannot at present prevent it.   But all
these inventions and discoveries are the gifts to mankind
of a virtuous, not a vicious genius.   They have added to
the world's blessings vastly more than to the world's
wretchedness and crimes.   By the use of them Faith
is outrunning doubt; Knowledge is blotting out ignorance; Health overcoming disease, and Righteousness
gaining advantage of Sin.   Soon, by these very facilities,
through which Vice is making such rapid growth, Vice
itself shall be mastered, when the country will enter a
new heavens and a new earth, wherein dwelleth righteousness.

The church has never been so fully equipped to
meet any crisis as she is to-day.   The world believes in
the divinity of her mission, so she can leave the defensive
and enter on the widest aggressive work.   ·She *is* aggressive.   Her forces are united, and they are moving into
every town and section of the land.   They are preaching the gospel "to every creature."   They are waiting at
Castle Garden to redeem the emigrant; building Bethels
to reach the sailor from the seas and the lakes, and the
boatmen on our streams.   They are waiting in "Way-

farers' Inns" and " Missions," to catch the drunken men and the fallen women from the "down-town wards" of our great cities; they are hewing their way among the pineries of the North; delving among the miners of the hills and mountains; in the South, they are reclaiming the negro, and in the West, the emigrant and the Indian. This whole land is surrounded and permeated through and through by lines of Christian watchfires, so that, if ten righteous men would have saved Sodom, we are, beyond a doubt, safe in the hands of our Christian forces.

Among the young men in American institutions of learning, the average as to character has never been so high. Indeed, outside of home, there is no place where it is so safe for parents to have their boys as in an American college.

Professor Shaler of Harvard says—" The student of to-day is a vast moral improvement over the student of thirty years ago."

In 1813, Princeton had three church members; now over one-half are enrolled Christians.

At Williams, of the two hundred and eighty-six students, one hundred and fifty-eight are church members.

At Amherst, two hundred and thirty-three out of three hundred and fifty-eight are in the church. Over one-half of the students at Bowdoin are connected with the college Young Men's Christian Association. In 1795, Yale had but four or five professing Christians, and the atmosphere was decidedly sceptical, but in the academic department in 1886-7, of the five hundred and seventy-four enrolled two hundred and forty-seven were members of evangelical churches.

Four hundred and twenty of the five hundred and fifty students at Wellesley College are members of the Christian Association and have signed the pledge, thus declaring their belief in Jesus Christ their Lord and Saviour, and dedicating their lives to His service.

In Iowa College, out of twenty-four seniors twenty-three are Christians; out of thirty-four juniors twenty-seven are Christians; out of fifty-four sophomores, fifty-

two; and out of sixty-two freshmen, fifty; and all in the
last two graduating classes.

Five colleges in Georgia, in 1887, graduated one
hundred and fourteen young men, ninty-four of whom
were professors of religion. In Park College, Missouri,
almost every student is a Christian.

The March number of the Monthly' Bulletin of the
University of Michigan, states that of the one thousand
five hundred and sixty-three pupils in all departments in
that University, eight hundred and five are professing
Christians. Of the two thousand one hundred and
thirty-one students in Presbyterian Colleges in the
United States, one thousand four hundred and fifteen
are church members. Six hundred of the twelve hundred young men in the nine colleges of Virginia are members of the Young Men's Christian Association. The interest among the students of the country in Foreign Mission work is truly wonderful, and omens well for the
future. Two of Princeton's young men have been making a canvass of our colleges and seminaries for the names
of pupils willing to become foreign missionaries. They
have heard from ninety-two institutions, and in these
are one thousand five hundred and twenty-five persons
who are willing to go to a foreign field, all but three
hundred of whom are young men.

These facts are given in such full details, because they
help us take our bearings, to know just where we are in
our search for the lost young man.

It has been referred to as a discouraging omen that
so many of our people are crowding into our cities.

From the census report of 1880, we learn that
thirteen million of our fifty millions, are in cities ranging
from four thousand population upward, i. e., more than
one-fourth, taking the country at large. But in the
older states, the proportion is much greater. More than
half of New York's five millions are in her cities and more
than one-fifth in the city of New York alone. In Connecticut more than one-half are in cities; so it is in New
Jersey, and nearly the same in Maryland; Massachusetts

has twice as many people in her cities as in the country. By 1890, Chicago alone will have one-fourth of the entire population of Illinois, and Philadelphia one-fourth of the great state of Pennsylvania.

The young men of the country are crowding into our cities more than any other class; thousands of them are leaving their homes to try their fortunes alone in the stores, workshops, and professions of the city; in doing so, it is agreed that they expose themselves far beyond what they do by remaining in the country. They come where vice is gilded, and so greatly more alluring; they are thrown into contact with clubs and associations, and so lose something of their independence, and come more under the spell of association. The attractions of the low theatres and of the saloons abound on every hand. How can a young man change from the country to the city without vastly increasing the risks of losing his immortal soul? This reasoning appears plausible, and has passed almost without questioning; but I venture to join issue, and affirm that the young man is better off, both materially and spiritually, in our American cities than in the country. The country is not the harmless place it is considered by many to be; human nature is no better out among the farms than in among the streets. Any one who has spent his boyhood days in a country school house, knows that the tempter is there with his wares, vending them without the refinements and blandishments thrown round sin in city life. Taking all things into account, it is far more safe to bring up a family of children in the city than in the country. There is more vice in the city, but there is more virtue. The stimulants to do right are a hundred fold increased; there are more appeals to our manhood; higher ideals are set before us; more eyes are watching us, and more voices calling to us to aspire and attain.

The best of everything has always been in the city: the best preachers, the best physicians, best lawyers, best schools, best churches. In music, amusements, social exchanges, opportunities to advance, the city has everything; the country almost nothing. It has been said that our city people would degenerate, if fresh blood did not flow in from the country. But it must be remembered that whilst many of our distinguished men have come from the farms, they have been *made* by the city, just as the ore, coming from the quiet hillsides, is in the city foundries and shops transformed into articles for universal use.

The great problems of our times are to be met and solved in the cities. The forces in the conflict are centering there. The seven cities of Chicago, Buffalo, Brooklyn, Pittsburg, Philadelphia, New York and Cincinnati, alone, have supplied more than one-sixth of the membership of the Northern Presbyterian Church, and more than one-third of the money spent in Home and Foreign Missions.

Let the young men come; a splendid army stands ready to surround them, and it will save them just as soon as we. learn how to dispose of and utilize our forces.

The church has put into the field two new divisions, that are already doing effective service; it is the Christian Woman and the Christian Young Man. Woman has better timber in her than was ever dreamed of in human philosophy; she has proven herself fully capable of supplying men's place in the industries of the world; she is just as good at one end of the telephone as the young man is at the other. As young men are dropping out as clerks, salesmen, treasurers, on account of their dissipations, women are taking their places, and filling them with as much ability, and more integrity; if all the young men of the land were to go on a prolonged spree, our women would man the old ship, and steer us over the rapids.

To the Christian woman we are looking for the toning up of the great underlying principles of personal and national life. She is, by example and heroic practice, teaching us the doctrines of a higher, holier service; she is making man's character more temperate, more pure, more Christ-like. What reform and redemption owe to such women as those who now fill the ranks of the Woman's Christian Temperance Union will never be known, till the day God takes some of the brightest crowns of his royal realm, and places them on their heads. To-day they surround our young men like a cloud of shining witnesses, and the voices of the best mothers, wives, daughters and sisters the world has ever seen are calling to them to run with patience the race set before them, and those voices will yet be heard. From every plea, and song, and prayer, hope springs like a white-winged seraph.

"Similia similibus curantur."

That means, similars cure similars; it is the motto of the Homeopath, under which he expects to cure a disease by administering remedies that in the proving produce symptoms similar to the symptoms of the disease. Whether this is a correct principle in medicine or not, is a matter of dispute among the schools. But the motto holds the secret of success in other departments of life; and it is in obedience to this that the church is to-day sending the young man to save the young man. The difficulty with the church heretofore, in her dealings with young men, is that she has not understood them, and so has failed to adapt her work to them.

The average young man, I may say the normal young man, is a creature of his own kind. At a certain period in his later boyhood, two marked movements take place in him: he begins to develop a certain form of physical manhood, and to become conscious of himself. Both are to be marvellous factors in his future usefulness and happiness, provided they are carefully handled. They have generally not been carefully handled, hence manhood has been so often blighted in the bloom. At this stage of his life the young man is not characterized for his taste for religious things. It is other elements in him that are coming forward. He has an exalted opinion of himself; this is said in all seriousness,

for it is true. He thinks much about his shape, his pos-
tures, his dress, his toilet. He is noisy about his home,
on the streets, and in the school; he sings, shouts,
says silly things, and does silly things. He is a "hale
fellow well met"; fastens himself to his companions, and
so they move, like fish in shoals. He is sensitive and
proud, takes offense easily, and demands more than ordinary attention from others. Just at this point you
may make a friend of him for life by a tip of the hat, or
a foe by an unintentional slight. One thing the young
man loves is " fun"; he must have it, and he will have it,
as the thirsty man will have water; if not furnished him
at home he will find it elsewhere; if not provided in
healthful places of resort, he is likely to take it in sinful
places.

Now in all these traits the young man is simply his
natural self; those of us who are mature, know that
it is a perfect description of ourselves at that period of
life. It is all right; God is doing His own work in the
young man, but we grow impatient with him, meet him
with a laugh and a jest, mortify him, and so alienate him
from the ways of progressive manhood. The proper thing
for us to do is to take him just as he is, and adapt our
methods to him; but this is a thing we have not done. The
pulpit and Sunday school books have dosed him with
lectures on sobriety and propriety until he is sick of them.
They have depreciated and abused his amusements till he
thinks the Kingdom of Heaven is not a place for the
merry-hearted, and so he prefers to stay out of it. They
keep thundering away at him for going to places of
doubtful resort, and have no better places of resort to
offer him.

The church is coming to her senses. We have
found that the best person to send for a young man, is
a Christian young man. This Christian young man has
not gotten over all the freshness of his early manhood
himself. He still has a good opinion of himself, but that
is one of his qualifications for his task. He still possesses
his love for fun, and that is another qualification. He

wants his devotional services short and sweet, and that is another. He still retains his aspirations as a gymnast and athlete. The bicycle and football are yet in his visions. His piety is robust and full of manly vigor. Half the devotion of a religious song lies in singing it loud and strong. He goes at his religion, as well as at his dumb-bells, with a " Hurrah, boys, hurrah!" He is just the man for the hour. Like Queen Esther, he has come to the kingdom for such a time as this. We have said to him, "go"; and look at the splendid association he has already built up; at the grand temples for young men that he has erected; and the sources of clean, hallowed, christianized entertainment and pastimes he has provided. The "Year Book of the Young Men's Christian Associations" of 1888, was a revelation to me. As I looked over, its pages, and saw how these Associations, manned by as consecrated worshipers as any the church possesses, has already gotten hold of thousands of our young men, in the hearts of merchandise, in the workshops, and along our rivers and railways, and have surrounded them with the brightness, cheer and refinement of elegant homes, I felt the country is safe. It is an illustration of the natural perversity of our nature that such a movement for the reclaiming of young men should be suspected and quietly opposed by some good people. But it has been the fate of all reforms. This, like others, will win its way to triumph, and the day is not far distant when Christian men and philanthropists will be just as zealous in having an elegant Young Men's Christian Association building in every town and city, as in having the school house and church.

How can I better close this chapter than in Whit tier's words, taken from "The Human Sacrifice"·

"As on the white sea's charmed shore
   The Parsee sees his holy hill,
With dunnest smoke—clouds curtained o'er,
Yet knows beneath them evermore,
   The low pale fire is quivering still ;
So, underneath its clouds of sin,
   The heart of man retaineth yet

Gleams of its holy origin;
　　And half quenched stars that never set,
D m colors of its faded bow
　　And early beauty, linger there,
And o'er its wasted desert blow
　　Faint breathings of the morning air,
O, never yet upon the scroll
Of the sin-stained, but priceless soul
　　Hath Heaven inscribed "*Despair.*"

CHAPTER VII.

A WORD TO THE WISE.

Appliances and organizations are important factors
in the work of reform, but they will prove powerless, and
hope will be turned to despair, if our young men remain
unwilling to do something for themselves. Their own
wills are the sovereigns in the shaping of their destiny.
We can transform marble without its consent, but not
a soul. A soul is not infinite, but it can thwart the
Infinite by simply saying "I will not." Young men
must cast aside the foolish excuses they make for their
wrong-doing, and turn toward the future with serious
purposes and manly resolves. It is a childish plea that
I hear so many make—we are so greatly tempted, and it
is hard to resist. Of course they are greatly tempted;
but who is there that is not? Temptations have always
existed and they have never come easy to any one.
Adam and Eve found them in the very Garden of Eden.
Christ met Satan in the wilderness where He had retired
for meditation. The pious Monks of the Primitive
Church retired into the caves and the wilderness, to escape the fascinations of social life, only to find that retire-
ment had its own allurements, and could transform the
unwary into the corrupt and vicious. It is very doubtful
whether the reasons for a young man's fall are any
greater to-day than they have ever been. There may
be in our age greater blandishments thrown around
the tempter than at any former period. He is dressed

better; is better educated; sings better; plays better; understands better the arts of approach and persuasion; lives amid more gaudy surroundings, and fares more sumptuously every day. But virtue is also better adorned, and more easy and graceful in her appeals. There never were such inducements as now for a young man to resist temptation and make a nobleman of himself.

The avenues open toward position and influence are innumerable. In this country all these avenues are free. Boys from the most humble homes and employments are rising every day to sway the scepters of our country. Rail-splitters, and canal-boatmen, and tanners, are becoming Presidents. The sons of blacksmiths, and carpenters, and printers are being transformed in a single generation into clergymen, and lawyers, and editors of distinction. Within a quarter of a century even slaves have sprung into prominence, and from high places are helping give shape to the education and to the laws of the land. With a future of such glorious promise, the young man who turns aside into the life of the sinning, and takes pleasure in the resorts of the fallen, is supremely foolish. It is never manly to submit to temptation, no matter how strong it may be, and no matter how dark the future may seem. A noble soul resists evil because it is right to do so, and the more determined his enemy is to subdue him, the more resolute is he to overcome. Daniel in Babylon was in exile; he was a child of a hated race; the worshiper of a despised divinity. He was in the hands of a tyrant who could take life at his pleasure. But what cared he for all this? He determined to separate himself from the splendid vices of a splendid court and did it. He did not plead the power of the temptation. It was the strength of the inducement that proved the strength of the young man. He could say No to a king, for he was more than a king; he was a child of God. To such a young man even fire has no terror, and a lion's mouth is only a way to freedom. Oh, for more of the heroism of the Hebrew captive among the young men

of our day.   One million such characters would transform our country in a single generation, and make us, in
private and public life, a God-fearing people.

There is a character in the Old Testament which I have
greatly admired, and which I am tempted to introduce,
as a model for young men, in the closing of this little
work.   It is Joshua, "a young man." Joshua stands
out as one of the three great men in the dawn of the
Hebrew national life.   The others are Moses and Aaron.
Of the three, the character of Joshua is most symmetrical.
Moses smote the rock instead of speaking to it as he
was commanded to do.   It is a recorded blemish in a
marvellous career.   Aaron, while Moses was in the mount,
united with the murmuring people, and bowed down to
the golden calf.   It was worse than a blemish — it was
an act of anarchy.

In the life of Joshua there is not a recorded fault.
He is one of the most pure and evenly-balanced characters of the whole Bible.   Nor does his faultlessness
arise from a lack of strength, for he has all those sturdy
positive traits that make him a successful soldier.   He
is just that kind of a man who finds temptation attractive, and who stands only by self-mastery.

No young man begins life as low down as did
Joshua.   His parents were Egyptian slaves, and for
more than forty years he was a slave himself.   The reasons for his laying violent hands on himself were abun-
dant, and the motives for his not doing it were few.
Yet there is evidence that amid all his discouragements
and hardships, he keeps himself as free from the contam-
inations of Egypt, as Daniel did afterward from those
of Babylon.   When, in the Exodus, Moses desired a leader
to go out to war against Amalek, it was Joshua that was
called to the front; when he desired "a young man" to
remain by his side as his private counsellor, it was Joshua
that was called to be his "minister."   When Israel chose
twelve men, heads of tribes, to spy out the promised
land, it was Joshua that was selected to represent his
tribe.

And when Moses was about to die, who should be his successor but Joshua.   Of course it was Joshua.   No one dreamed of any other to take the high place vacated by death.   God did not dream of any other; if He had selected another, the people would have said they could have done better themselves.   In every crisis moment, where God is shaping events, the best man gets to the front.   It is no hap-hazard selection.   God chooses His men for high responsibilities, just as men choose them. He selects those who have been tested and have proven themselves worthy.

God always has positions for the young men who honor Him and do His commandments.   The fact is, all life's honorable positions are God's places, and it is He that is laying hands on men to fill them.   Abraham Lincoln was as much God's man as was Moses or Joshua. He selected him for a critical moment and a critical task. So was Grant God's man; so was Edwin M. Stanton. The average young man of to-day thinks God has nothing to do with success in life; hence it is he keeps away from His altar, and cares nothing for the "clean hands" and the "pure heart" that come through compassing it.

We sometimes speak of there being a charm in these Joshuas.   Some "divinity" shapes their "ends" that is not granted to most men.   In common parlance it is called "luck."   But the only charm and luck are those that are at the command of every young man who is determined to make the best out of himself.   It is the "charm" every true man throws round his fellow men and the "luck" of a good Father in Heaven who stands by and helps every man who does nobly to help himself. The truth is, what are called "lucky" men in this world are not often the successful men.   Those who are born of wealthy parents, and have men in high position to give them a favorable start in life, are considered the favorites of the Goddess of Fortune.   But when one calls the roll of the great, it is remarkable how few of these high-born young men respond.   Their start in life was too high for them.   They grew up the pets of wealthy households;

constant indulgence led many of them into temptation, and they fell, and great was their fall. Many who succeeded in preserving their morals, came into life without self-reliance, so that when some crisis arose, as it will arise with every young man, in which he must stand by his own strength, they failed because their good fortune made them weak. Fortune, the fair goddess, seems to favor the young men who begin life at the foot of the ladder. Certain it is, at least, that the ladder, whose foot is on the earth, and its top amid the clouds, presents the strange sight of ascending and descending columns. The children of the great coming down and the children of the lowly going up, the first becoming last and the last first. Such a condition of things should not be. Those who begin life in high places should not descend simply because they have had the assistance of others, and,they will not, when they learn that self-restraint and self-reliance are as becoming to the high-born as the low-born. But, at the present stage of human progress, it is the fact that the " ups " of one generation become the " downs " of the next, and the " downs " the " ups."

Gov. Palmer of Illinois was once a country blacksmith; so was Robert Collier once a knight of the anvil.

Erastus Corning of New York began life as a shop boy in Albany. He was lame and so could do no very hard work. When he made his application for employment, he was asked, " Why, my little fellow, what can you do? " "Can do what I am bid," was his reply, which secured him the place. Senator Wilson of Massachusetts was a shoe-maker; Thurlow Weed, a canal-boat driver.

Ex-Gov. Stone of Iowa and Hon. Stephen A. Douglas both sprang from the homes of cabinet makers.

What has interested me most, in the case of Joshua, is the secret of his steady rise from a bondman to the position of the leader of the Hebrews. The secret after all is no secret at all. It is what has made all Joshuas great. It is what will make all our young men successful if they are willing to fall into line, and follow the counsel of the wise.

Joshua kept his character above suspicion. He indulged in none of the social extravagances and vices of his day, held no loose views of morality that led him into "early indiscretions," consorted with none of the wild and gay young fellows around him. The Bible does not tell us these things; but we know they must have been so, for they are always true of the men who march without a halt from the lowly beginnings of life to their glorious endings. It is the height of folly for a young man, if he desires to succeed, to soil his reputation by any kind of wrong doing. A spotless character is the very best capital with which to begin life. It is a thousand times better than money: for money may fly away in a day, but character stays for life, if its possessor does not choose himself to destroy it.

Years ago Arthur Tappan was prominent as a merchant in New York city. He was equally notorious for his opposition to slavery and for his personal integrity. Rev. E. A. Rand in the *Golden Rule* represents a fellow merchant of Tappan as saying, "If Arthur Tappan will allow his name to be put on my store and will sit in an arm-chair in my counting room, I will pay him three thousand dollars a year." Here was a living salary for a character. Now, character is within the reach of every boy. He need not spend money to possess it; he need not ascend into heaven to bring it down nor descend into the depths to bring it up. It comes, it grows; it is inevitable, if a boy will begin life by always doing right. It will not be a question, when he seeks a position, whether men will respect him. That is settled at the start. Character is always respected; even those who have none of their own, bow down to it.

In a public life of twenty-five years, I have met hundreds of young men who could not find a place, and it was no wonder to me. They had done nothing to deserve a place; indeed, they had done everything to destroy their desert for position by smirching their reputation in loose ways of living. Some of them had done wrong on the "sly" and seemed surprised that they

were so well known. They found out to their sorrow
that all sinning works to the surface like the needle that
is buried in the flesh. In these twenty-five years, I have
never met a worthy young man who was long without
a position. The world needs him and will use him when
he is ready. Positions seem to spring out of the soil
for him. He can scarcely tell how they come; but they
come and stay with him. It is surprising how many
men of large possessions and extensive responsibilities
are on the still-hunt for young men of character. I have
even known of detectives being sent out to make inquiries concerning persons whose fame had extended beyond the limits of their own home.

Admiral Farragut's estimate of a good character as
a business investment may be learned in the account he
gives of his start in life. He says:

"My father was sent down to New Orleans with the
little navy we then had, to look after the treason of Burr.
I accompanied him as cabin boy, and was ten years of
age. I had some qualities which I thought made a man
of me. I could swear like an old salt; could drink a
stiff glass of grog as if I had doubled Cape Horn, and
could smoke like a locomotive. I was great at cards,
and fond of gaming of every shape. At the close of the
dinner, one day, my father turned everybody out of the
cabin, locked the door, and said to me: 'David, what do
you mean to be?' 'I mean to follow the sea.' 'Follow
the sea! Yes, be a poor miserable drunken sailor before
the mast, kicked and cuffed about the world, and die in
some fever hospital in a foreign clime.' 'No,' I said; 'I'll
tread the quarter-deck, and command as you do.' 'No,
David, no boy ever trod the quarter-deck with such
principles as you have, and such habits as you exhibit.
You'll have to change the whole course of your life if
you ever become a man.'

"My father left me and went on deck. I was
stunned by the rebuke, and overwhelmed with mortifi-
cation. 'A poor, miserable, drunken sailor before the
mast, kicked and cuffed about the world, and to die in

some fever hospital! That's my fate, is it? I'll change my life, and change it at once. I will never utter another oath; I will never drink another drop of intoxicating liquor; I will never gamble.' And as God is my witness, I have kept those three vows to this hour. Shortly after I became a Christian. That act settled my destiny for time and eternity."

In the records of his life, I see no evidence that Joshua was ever impatient with his position, nor restless because he could not advance more rapidly. With him, his successive promotions came slowly. He was about forty-five years old before he became a free man. It is at this age that he is still called "a young man." For thirty-nine years longer, he was content to serve in subordinate positions. The crowning glory of his lifetime,—his succeeding to the place held by Moses,—came to him at the advanced age of eighty-four years.

In our era there are few who consider themselves "young men" at forty-five. By that time, many are dead; many who live are worn out, and are the wrecks of their former manhood. Well preserved men are not yet in their prime at fifty. I have been told that in England sixty is considered the age at which the climax of one's powers is reached; that after that, this high state of ability is maintained till seventy-five, when there begins a graceful, honorable decline of from five to ten years. This gives a young man, starting in business, a long period in which to accumulate wealth and glory. But the average young man is not willing to wait. He wants to go up with a rush. Tell him that he may still be a poor man at forty-five, and he will give up in despair. Life will not be worth living. He wants to get married, and how can he keep a wife until he has an independent income. The place he has started in is too humble; it does not pay him a sufficient salary; he cannot meet his social expenses on his income. He grows restless, and because reckless, unreliable; his employer ceases to trust him, and, instead of rising, he is in the condition of the dog in the fable, which lost the meat in his mouth by trying to grasp its shadow in the water.

A little common sense, and a little more contentment, will reveal to the young man in a lowly station, that promotion need not be so tardy as he suspects. If there are twenty persons between him and the place in the establishment which he covets, he will find, if he waits, that not the half of them will be patient for advancement, but will disappear in pursuit of better places, so that, at the start, there are really not ten men who stand in front of him. Of these few, the older ones, in time, will either retire or die, and their positions must be filled. Promotion is certain, if one is only patient: and it will come often and be great, if he will not think he must grow old at fifty, and must retire from business at fifty-five.

As I look over the lives of eminent men, I find that the vast majority of them never reached the climax of their success till comparatively late in life.

Samuel Morse was over fifty years old before he could persuade the American people that there was anything in his proposed Telegraph.

Buffon was forty-two before he published his "Natural History." The height of his fame as a Naturalist was not reached till he was over sixty; and at seventy he was still hard at work on his " Epochs of Nature." He gives the secret of his success when he says: "*Genius is Patience.*"

William Carey was still a cobbler at thirty; at forty he had not yet made himself master of the Sanskrit and Bengalee. At the time of life when many want to retire, he was advancing to a professorship in the College of Fort William, and to the glory of being the translator of the Scriptures into several oriental languages. When asked to explain how he ever rose from the bench of a shoemaker to become a scholar, he replied: "*I can plod.*"

The fame of Benjamin Franklin did not begin to be world-wide till he was fifty. He was seventy years old before he had the honor of appending his name to the Declaration of Independence. He was eighty-two before he became a delegate to the Convention called to form the Federal Constitution. When he died at eighty-four, twenty thousand people assembled to do honor to his remains; while everywhere, in Europe and America, the highest eulogiums were uttered in his memory. The secret of his success was a simple one. He gave it thus: "*My rule is to go straight on in doing what appears to me to be right, leaving the consequences to Providence.*"

The great element in the building up of Joshua's character was his faith in God. This faith was more to him than a simple salve to save his soul, or a couch on which he might rest easy in his death. It was an indwelling and inspiring force, and served him in all the movements of his life. It was this, more than anything else, that made him honorable and reliable in positions of trust. Duty was done under the high motive that it pleased God. His faith made him patient and contented, for it taught him that the Lord was his Shepherd, and would care for him. It made him brave in battle, for it assured aim that with God is victory. His estimate of the Christian Faith as a help in the ordinary pursuits of life, is given in his address at the close of his life: " One of you shall chase a thousand; for the Lord your God, He it is that fighteth for you."

The presence of an infinite God, binding Himself by solemn promises to protect and assist those who put their trust in Him; the coming of a great Divine Spirit into the souls that are open to receive Him, making their bodies the " temples of the Holy Ghost," are the most lofty and inspiring thoughts that can enter the minds of men. There is nothing in human poetry or philosophy to approach it in sublimity. Such convictions, so lodged in the soul as to possess it, must expand its out-look, exalt its motives, and fill it with enthusiasm, as nothing else can.

Yet the Christian even makes little out of his faith

as an every-day working power; while most of our
young men never dream of taking it into account. God
is no more to them than if He had no existence; and His
promises fall on their ears like the babblings of childhood. Indeed, the religious life seems to the average
young man as a silly, unmanly mummery; it is beneath
his high ideas of manhood. He places himself on the
back seat in a religious meeting, with the air of a nobleman, deigning to halt for a moment to look at some
boyish sport. With him, it is "smart" to doubt, and
to profess infidelity. Such conduct might amuse the
wise and great, if it were not so serious. It becomes a
matter of the deepest sorrow, when we look on it as
youth throwing out of its preparation for life, the only
element that will insure him success, and the only Being
who can save the soul.

There is an idea prevailing to-day among thousands,
that no great men have been Christians. Surely those
who believe such a thing never read, for some of the
most devout of Christ's followers have come from the
ranks of the world's great.

Bismarck, the greatest diplomatist of his times, is a
humble, trusting disciple of Christ.

The nineteenth century has produced no greater
philosopher and metaphysician than Sir Wm. Hamilton
of Scotland. He was a master in every branch of
learning that he touched. Yet, "while at home in the
learning of all ages, and exciting the wonder of his con-
temporaries by the bold sweeps of his genius, no less
than the vastness of his attainments, he sat as a little
child at the feet of Jesus. He was a sincere believer.
There is an exquisite pathos in the record of his last
hours, that, when his spirit was hovering on the borders
of the unseen world, just ready to penetrate its mys-
teries, he was heard to murmur: 'Thy rod and Thy staff,
they comfort me.'"

Shakespeare wrote in nis will : " I commend my soul
into the hands of God my Creator, hoping, and assuredly
believing, through the only merits of Jesus Christ my

Saviour, to be made partaker of life everlasting, and my body to the earth whereof it is made."

These few words from the late Dr. J. G. Holland's will, reveal his grateful, loving, and religious spirit: " I am thankful for having enjoyed the privileges of labor and influence, thankful for wife and children, thankful for all my success. I have intentionally and consciously wronged no man, and if I know my own heart, I have forgiven all my enemies. For the great hereafter, I trust in the Infinite Love, as it is expressed to me in the life and death of my Lord and Saviour Jesus Christ."

Josiah Quincy, formerly President of Harvard College, lived to be ninety-two years of age. He had kept a journal for many years. He was accustomed to sit in the morning in a large chair with a broad arm to it, which served as a desk, upon which he wrote his diary. July 1st, 1864, he sat down in his chair as usual. His daughter brought his journal. He at first declined to undertake his wonted task, but his daughter urged him not to abandon it. He took the book, and wrote the first verse of that grateful hymn of Addison:

"When all thy mercies, O my God,
My rising soul surveys,
Transported by the view, I'm lost
In wonder, love, and praise."

The weary head dropped upon the bosom. The volume was ended. The soul had fled.

Daniel Webster, one of the greatest orators, statesmen and constitutional lawyers of the age, paid the following grand and noble tribute to the cause of our, Saviour: "Religion is a necessary, an indispensable element in any great human character. There is no living without it. It is the tie that connects man with his Creator and holds him to His throne. If that tie is sundered or broken, he floats away a worthless atom in the universe, its proper attractiveness all gone, its destiny thwarted, and its whole future but darkness, desolation and death."

No man more fittingly adorned the United States Senate and the Vice Presidency, in connection with General Grant, than Henry Wilson of Massachusetts. The conscientious fidelity to principle and duty which characterized his career as a mechanic, editor, State Senator, Chairman of the Committee on Military Affairs, and as reconstructionist of the Southern States, until he reached the highest office in the gift of his countrymen, was conspicuous in all his philanthropic and religious engagements. He belonged to the highest order of nobility God has on earth, and remained to the last one of His pillars in the temple of grace.

Speaking of his conversion, he used these words: "I have never shielded myself by infidelity, nor defended my position by that poorest of all excuses, the faults of professors. I now trust that in answer to the prayers of a departed wife and other friends now living I have found an abiding peace. I would not exchange the hope I have for any earthly honors. I have enjoyed more assurance and peace during the last week than in any other period of my life. I give myself and all I have and hope for to my Lord and Master. And if there has been anything kept back, I pray it may be shown me."

A gentleman who enjoyed a somewhat intimate acquaintance with Wendell Phillips, a quarter of a century ago, but had not met him for some years, gives the following incident in the Boston *Watchman:* "Renewing the acquaintance upon my return, I sought an interview within the past twelve months for the express purpose of learning his religious views. I opened the conversation by saying to him frankly that, in my absence, I had heard him quoted as skeptical as to the claims of Christ and His teachings, and asked of him as a friend, his statement of his present position in the matter. Turning to me his noble face and winning smile, he said: 'I believe in Jesus as the Saviour of lost men, and in His gospel as the revealed will of God for man's belief and acceptance. It is the word of life to a lost world.'"

The late Charles Reade, the novelist, it is said, wrote

his own epitaph, which is to be engraved upon a plain slab, to be placed upon his grave. It is as follows:

"Here lie, by the side of his beloved friend, the mortal remains of Charles Reade, dramatist, novelist and journalist. His last words to mankind are on this stone. I hope for a resurrection, not from any power in Nature, but from the will of the Lord God Omnipotent, who made Nature and me. He created man out of nothing, which Nature could not. He can restore man from the dust, which Nature cannot. And I hope for holiness and happiness in a future life, not for anything I have said or done in this body, but from the merits and mediation of Jesus Christ. He has promised His intercession to all who seek it, and He will not break His word. That intercession, once granted, cannot be rejected; for He is God, and His merits are infinite; a man's sins are but human and finite. 'Him that cometh to me, I will in no wise cast out.' 'If any man sin, we have an advocate with the Father, Jesus Christ the Righteous; and He is the propitiation for our sins.'"

President Porter of Yale College closed one of his baccalaureate sermons with these words:

"No sign of our times is more depressing than that so many refined and thoughtful young men so readily accept the suggestions of doubt and take a position of indifference or irresponsibility in respect to the truths of Christian theism and the personal obligations which they enforce." After warning his hearers against these tendencies, the President concluded: "I declare to you in this sacred place, as you look back upon your college life, and as you look hopefully forward to the unknown future, that if you would live a life of cheerful, joyful, aud buoyant hopefulness, you must live a life that is controlled and cheered and hallowed by God's presence, and by a constant faith in His forgiving goodness. All else that a man should care for is secured you by this living hope in the living and ever present God. All things are yours; ye are Christ's and Christ is God's. These are the traditions of this place. Under these influences the generations have been trained which have gone before, each testifying that the truth and instructions, of which perhaps they had been more or less heedless while here, have come again to them with living power when recalled under the experiences of life. So may it ever be; so may it be with you. With these wishes and this blessing do I bid you an affectionate farewell."

I clip the following from one of our periodicals of recent date:

"If Christianity cannot stand the sifting of modern criticism and the cool common sense of the nineteenth century, we ought to find it abandoned by business men who have no interest in maintaining a religious delusion, and who are supposed to be hard-headed and keen in the detection of imposture. But a census taken in the city of Minneapolis shows that of the three hundred and ninety-one owners and officers of the eighty-two largest business concerns, two hundred and eighty-six are professing Christians, ninety-four are favorable to Christianity, and eleven are opposed to it; or, putting it differently, three per cent. of the whole number are opposed to Christianity, twenty-four per cent. are favorable, and seventy-three per cent. are personally believers on the Lord Jesus Christ. Similar inquiries in other cities show similar results. The one who says that Christianity is losing its hold on 'practical men' does not know what he is talking about."

These numerous instances are given in hope that the young men who may read them may be convinced that it is altogether consistent with the highest manhood and the proudest attainments for them to be Christians.

At one hundred and ten years of age Joshua died. It is always intensely interesting to know how great men die; and to see whether the philosophy of their lives support them to the close. The belief that one cannot die with, is a poor one to live with. It shakes the faith of the sceptic in the theories of Voltaire, when he learns that the old scoffer in his last sickness, made a profession of faith in God, and died in the membership of the Catholic church.

Who wants to commit himself to the infidelity of Hume, the English historian, when he finds him closing his earthly career with " I am affrighted and confounded with that forlorn solitude into which I am placed by my philosophy, and fancy myself some uncouth, strange monster, who, not being able to mingle and unite in society, has been expelled all human commerce, and left utterly abandoned and disconsolate?"

The death of Joshua was as sublime as his life. His faith in God was never more triumphant. It had led him to exclaim on the battle-field, as he took God at His promise, "Sun, stand thou still upon Gibeon; and thou, moon, in the valley of Ajalon." Now, facing the eternal world, it brings him a marvellous repose. Like a man starting on some ordinary mission, he says, " Behold, this day I am going the way of all the earth." " I am going!" Is that all dying is?

Roscoe Conkling seemed to think otherwise, for in his eulogy over Oliver P. Morton, delivered in the senate chamber, he said:

" Death is nature's supreme abhorrence. The dark valley, with its weird and solemn shadows, illumined by the rays of Christianity, is still the ground which man shudders to approach. The grim portals and the narrow house seem in the lapse of centuries to have gained rather than lost in impressive and foreboding horror."

Joshua does not call death " the grim portals"; he says, " it is the way of all the earth." Earth's ways are not hard ways. No man " shudders to approach" them. First the sunshine, then the spring; first the spring, then the harvest; first the harvest, then the gladness of full garners and gratified homes. First the showers, then awakened and adorned verdure. First the day for business, then the night for rest. First childhood; then manhood and womanhood; then marriage and home; then an honorable and peaceful old age. These are earth's ways. " Going " in them is a constant blessedness.   If dying is simply "going the way of all the earth," then it is like all Nature's works, a consummation—a glorious translation.   •

Thus it is faith in God gives confidence and repose as one enters the door that sooner or later swings open for all.   It comes with the kindness of a mother "who wraps the drapery of the couch" around her weary child, laying him "down to pleasant dreams."

CPSIA information can be obtained
at www.ICGtesting.com
Printed in the USA
LVOW10s1107020917
547355LV00026B/284/P